At the Tip of the Boot
As told by a WWI POW

My Memory of My Imprisonment in Austria

"Hunger" Diary by

Fedele Loria, 1917

Roger G. Hill
Author / Translator / Transcriber

DP DIVERSIFIED
244 5th Ave Ste G-200
NY, NY 10001

At the Tip of the Boot: As told by a WWI POW
© 2023 by Roger G. Hill. All rights reserved.

Published by
DP Diversified
a division of
DocUmeant Publishing
NY, NY 10001
646-233-4366

Original Work Loria Fedele, 1917, Hunger; Author, Translator/Transcriber: Roger G. Hill

Editor: Anne C. Jacob
Digital images scanned and edited by: Robert Jacob
Cover by: Patti Knoles
Layout, and Design by: DocUmeant Designs' www.DocUmeantDesings.com

First Edition
Library of Congress Cataloging-in-Publication Data

Names: Loria, Fedele, 1896-1973 author. | Hill, Roger G., translator,
    compiler.
Title: At the tip of the boot : as told by a WWI POW, my memory of my
    Imprisonment in Austria / Loria Fedele ; translated and transcribed by
    Roger G. Hill.
Other titles: As told by a WWI POW, my memory of my Imprisonment in Austria

Description: [New York] : [DocUmeant Publishing], [2023] | Includes
    bibliographical references and index. | Summary: "In the darkest days of
    his life, Fedele Loria put a quill pen on paper and told his story. As a
    prisoner during the First World War, he was forced to experience every
    human emotion in the extreme. Despair and hopelessness overwhelm his
    companions on Christmas Eve 1917. We see hope for the future when he
    says, "So many times have I dreamed of my beautiful liberty." He tells
    us in his diary about the mundane daily life in a concentration camp. He
    describes to us the poignant and touching last hours of his mortally
    wounded friend. The depth of his thoughts, his faith in God, his love of
    family, and his deeply felt compassion, are woven into the fabric of his
    writing"-- Provided by publisher.
Identifiers: LCCN 2023012600 | ISBN 9781950075966 (hardcover)
Subjects: LCSH: Loria, Fedele, 1896-1973--Diaries. | World War,
    1914-1918--Concentration camps--Austria. | World War,
    1914-1918--Prisoners and prisons. | Prisoners of war--Italy. | Prisoners
    of war--Austria. | Mauthausen (Concentration camp) | Loria family. |
    Loria, Fedele, 1896-1973--Family. | Italian Americans--West
    Virginia--Genealogy. | San Giovanni in Fiore (Italy)--Genealogy.
Classification: LCC D627.A8 L588 2023 | DDC 940.54/72436092
    [B]--dc23/eng/20230522
LC record available at https://lccn.loc.gov/2023012600

To My Loving Wife, Marie,

who has dedicated her life and unending loyalty to me and our sons Joe and Jonny. This book is dedicated to them. I could never have written it without the support and encouragement of my sons and my dear wife.

I love you, Marie Bridges Hill.

When you have a passion
combined with a
deep love for an endeavor,
there comes to mind
a time-worn phrase:
"It is a labor of love."
So it is with me, this book,
and that old worn phrase.

Roger G. Hill

2023

Contents

Part I
Contents of the Diary
with Translation and Commentary

Part II
Documentation

Part III
Considering the Past, Present, and Future

Figures

Preface

IN THE DARKEST days of his life, Fedele Loria put a quill pen on paper and told his story. As a prisoner during the First World War, he was forced to experience every human emotion in the extreme. Despair and hopelessness overwhelm his companions on Christmas Eve 1917. We see hope for the future when he says, "So many times have I dreamed of my beautiful liberty." He tells us in his diary about the mundane daily life in a concentration camp. He describes to us the poignant and touching last hours of his mortally wounded friend. The depth of his thoughts, his faith in God, his love of family, and his deeply felt compassion, are woven into the fabric of his writing.

I doubt Fedele ever dreamed that more than a hundred years later, his descendants would read his account of the time when he was a prisoner in Austria. After the war, Fedele returned to America. Most likely, he forgot about the diary that he left in the closet of his parents' house in Calabria. Fedele rarely spoke of his experiences in wartime. He may have forgotten the book, but the things he saw, the things he did, and the hell he lived through, could never have completely left him.

This long forgotten and nearly lost piece of family history has now come to light. The story in his diary is a part of our family history. It deserves to be preserved as the precious family heirloom that it is. We owe it to him to remember his name, his life, and his story.

This book is not meant to be a complete biography about the life and times of Fedele. The focus will be on that period of his life between the ages of fifteen and twenty-three. This is a book about his book. He told his story, and I am preserving it. Come along with me on a journey to explore the man, his thoughts, and his words. He wrote it in short sessions. Taking in his book a bit at a time allowed me to understand his thoughts and feelings on more than a superficial level.

We all have a philosophy of life. Some of us think about it more than others. Most people need an entire lifetime to know themselves and their core beliefs. War and captivity brought clarity to Fedele's philosophy of life and his core beliefs before the age of twenty-three. At such a young age, he may not have given much thought to his legacy. Whether he intended to or not, he did leave a legacy. Fedele had his faith in God, hope for the future, and a deep love of family.

By showing us these core beliefs in writing, he has left us a priceless legacy. We know what mattered most to him. He learned these things from his ancestors. Even if you have never thought about it, keep in mind that all of us will be ancestors. Your values and your core beliefs will be how you are remembered. Don't just leave a memory. Make a mark. Be the influence that will live on for generations after your name is forgotten.

"Leave a legacy that money can't buy, and taxes cannot take away."
—Steven J. Lawson

I have had sixty-seven years to think about these things. Carefully studying his diary has encouraged me to explore my beliefs and values. Some time spent in introspective thought has clarified what I believe and who I am. As a result, I have found some common ground with Fedele's philosophy of life. The beliefs we share are simple.

Know your roots, know yourself, leave a legacy.

Introduction

Figure 1: Fedele's passport photo

Who was Fedele Loria?

FEDELE LORIA WAS born into crushing poverty in Calabria, Italy, in 1896. The old hometown of San Giovanni in Fiore is in the "ankle of the boot" of Italy. In 1912, Fedele had two brothers and three uncles mining coal in West Virginia. His parents removed him from school and sent him to America, where he joined his brothers and uncles in the mines. Fedele was raised in The Catholic faith, and he had an immense love of family, country, and God. When WWI started, he and his two brothers volunteered to join the Italian infantry. His family sent him to America to do a dangerous job. Love of country brought the brothers back to Italy to do an even more dangerous job. Six months into the war, Fedele was severely wounded and captured by the Austrians. Eventually, he recovered from the surgery to repair his wounds. His captivity lasted for two years, four months, and three weeks.

The Austrians did their best to kill him on the battlefield. Later they tried to starve him and thousands of Italian prisoners to death. Sometimes they succeeded. The war ended in victory for Italy in November 1918. He was honorably discharged in December 1919. He and his brothers returned to their mother's home for some rest and relaxation and some of mom's cooking.

He knew there was no future for him in Italy as a farmer. Fedele and his brother Giovanni returned to the mines in May of 1920. Four years later, Fedele got married to Anna Marie Pedro. They reared nine children in Boomer, West Virginia. He came from poverty and raised himself and his family up to American middle-class standards. Fedele lived for seventy-three years, and then he succumbed to abdominal cancer. We can't be certain, but his cancer may have had its seed planted when he was exposed to mustard gas in the trenches. As a result of his life's efforts, immense sacrifices, and dedication to family, he now has eight grandchildren, twenty great-grandchildren, and two great-great-grandchildren. We will see in his diary that one man can make a difference for generations to come.

THE CALABRIAN DIALECT

Prior to 1861, Italy was comprised of twenty-one independent regions, each with its own dialect derived from Latin. After the unification of Italy in 1861, standardized Italian came into use throughout the country, including the schools. Fedele would have learned the Calabrian dialect as a child in the home. Later in school, he would learn standard Italian. The regional dialects are still used today at home or among close friends. We can be sure that when he was in WV with his relatives, they spoke in dialect. I do not speak Italian well, but I can get by in a conversation. During my visits to San Giovanni, I heard our cousins using the Calabrian dialect. I found it nearly impossible to understand a single word in spoken or written form. The difference would be comparable to someone with a Louisiana bayou accent talking to someone from the Bronx of New York.

Why Did He Write a Diary?

My friend, Larry Nerge, an Air Force veteran, shed some light on what all combat veterans experience. The one thing they all have in common is prolonged periods of boredom punctuated by moments of sheer terror. Whether they were in the trenches or in the prison camp, they felt the same fear, hunger, and pain as they slept shoulder to shoulder. Men in combat survive not just for themselves, they live so that they can defend the life of the man next to them in the mud. In these circumstances, men become closer to each other than they are to their own families. They share experiences and feelings that civilians could never understand. During the tedious hours in prison, they share stories of their youth, and talk about their wives, their children, and of course, their parents.

Fedele had a great capacity for compassion. He would have deeply felt the shared emotional trauma of being a combat-wounded veteran and a POW. He understood well that for all of them, home and hope were far away. You will see through his writing that he embraced the things they told him. Fedele internalized them and amplified the words of his prison mates.

This is not a memoir written in the twilight of life but a real-time snapshot of his experiences as he lived them. He was an eyewitness to history as it was being made.

Lost in Translation

Much of the diary is written as poetry with meter and rhythm. Some things just do not translate well, and poetry is one of them. According to my Italian friends, Aldo and Daniela, he used a style of poetry that was taught in school. His education ended at age fifteen. When possible, the translation is literally word for word. According to my Italian friends who have reviewed the diary, it is their opinion that, even with insightful commentary, much is lost in the translation.

Aldo and Daniela were invaluable when interpreting those misspelled words, hard-to-read script, and phrases in the Calabrian dialect. If you ask two people to interpret one sentence, you might get three answers. In a few passages, he uses words that are not in standard Italian or the Calabrian dialect. They are literally lost, and without translation. He wrote with a quill pen dipped in ink while using his own cursive style. Even native speakers struggle to read his handwriting. By anyone's measure, this diary is difficult to read and challenging to interpret.

Large parts of the writing are in the form of a narrative. I have struggled to relate his story without straying too far from the central idea. It was tempting to make some assumptions about what I believed he really meant to say. When translating some passages literally, the result often is nonsensical. A subjective translation of what most closely aligns with his central idea is easier said than done. The context seems to be the key here. By reading and re-reading the surrounding paragraphs, it is possible to gain a better understanding of his meaning and intent. Fedele uses literary devices such as sarcasm, metaphor, imagery, flashback, and hyperbole. Despite the challenge of reading and understanding his words, it is plain to see there was far more to his intellect than would be needed by an infantry soldier or a coal miner.

We see motives for self-preservation in his writing style. He had to have considered the risk of putting into writing a description of his circumstances. The Austrians tried to kill him quickly on the battlefield, and later they tried to slowly starve him in prison. In the entirety of his diary, he did not write a single derogatory word about the Austrians. The writing of his book would not likely have taken place in secrecy. The prison guards were watching, they would have seen him writing. He knew his book could be confiscated at any time, and his written words could be used against him. In the chapter, *Speech of the Prisoner*, he makes an oblique reference to punishment with an iron rod for speaking up. Some died by beatings. He had to be careful.

You will see his words exactly as he wrote them. Fedele was not a stickler for punctuation, spelling, or grammar. He uses poetic license to omit or condense words so that they fit the meter or rhyme as needed.

PART I

Contents of the Diary

with Translation and Commentary

John Frenk

— Mie memorie —
della mia

Prigionia in austria

« Kriegsgefangenen 117

N. 41925

Loria Fedele

Goding il 12/12/1917

John Frenk

Mie memorie

del la mio

Prigioniae in austria

Kriegsgefangenen 172

N. 41925

Loria Fedele

Goding 12/12/1917

John Frenk[1]

My memories

of my

Imprisonment in austria

Prisoner of war camp 172

N. 41925[2]

Loria Fedele[3]

Goding 12/12/1917[4]

Author Commentary

1. I have no idea why he would place the name, John Frenk, in the upper right corner.
2. His prisoner number is 41925.
3. It was customary to write one's signature with the last name then the first name.
4. Goding is a small town in southern Austria.

Sigmundscherberg N. Ö. 7

La lingua delle donne

Loria Fedele

1.00
6.0 0
3.0 0
3.0 0
2,1 ¾ Corona Ceccarelli
6 0, Centi Dimartino
30 Centi Martinelli 30 Centi Malesano

Sigmundscherberg. N.07

La lingua Delle donne

Loria Fedele

10.

5,0

3,0

3,0

21 7 Corana Ceccarelli

50 Centi Martino

30 Centi Martinelli

30 centi Malsano

Sigmundscherberg. N. 07[1]

The Tongue of women[2]

Loria Fedele.

10[3]

5.0

3.0

3.0

21 7 Corana Ceccarelli

50 Centi Martino

30 Centi Martinelli

30 centi Malsano[4]

Author Commentary

1. Sigmundscherberg. N. 07 is the name of a prison camp.
2. The language or the tongue of women
3. This could be money that he lent or borrowed along with the name of the other person.
4. I think this was a practice page with miscellaneous notes. Later, there is a poem titled "The language of women."

La Canzona del Prigioniero.

1ª

E Mauthausen quel Paese
Dove sono i Prigionieri
Io vlo dico questo é vero
Era meglio di morire,

2ª

La Polenta é quella cosa
Che mangiavo una volta l'anno.
Invece qui quando la danno
Una gran festa gli si fa'.

3ª

La Patata le quel frutto
Che si cava sotto terra.
Ci voleva questa Guerra.
Per patata diventar

La Canzona del Prigioniero

"Quante Volte lo Sognato la mia Bella Libertà"

The Song of the Prisoner

"How Many Times Have I Dreamed of my Beautiful Liberty"

1a

E Mauthausen quell Paese
Dove sono I Prigionieri
Io lo dico questo e' vero
Era meglio di morire.

1a

This region is Mount Hausen

Where we are prisoners

I tell you this is true

It was better than to die.

2a

La Polenta e'quella cosa
Che mangiavo una volta l'anno.
Invece qui quando la danno
Unna gran festa gli si fa'

2a

Polenta is the thing

We used to eat once a year.

Here/now/when they give it to us

One has a great celebration.

3 a

La patata le quell frutto
che si cova sotto terra.
Ci Voleva questa guerra
Per patate diventar

3a

The potatoes are that fruit

that you pull from underground.

we needed this war

to become potatoes.

Author Commentary

1. Conditions at Mauthausen concentration camp were horrible, but it was better than dying.
2. In Calabria, polenta was rarely eaten. Corn for polenta is grown in northern Italy, not in the south. It would have been an expensive treat.
3. While living in the trenches, a lot of time was spent underground in the dirt. When Fedele was captured he was pulled from the muddy trenches and put into cold storage in the Alps, as if he and the other prisoners were potatoes.

4ª

Stoccafisso con merluzzo
Sono Pesci dano o mare
Indee qui dobbiamo mangiare
Tutti i giorni Baccalà

5ª

L'arrenga che quel pesce
Che mangiado assai di rado
Indee qui Tutto a stufato
Pesce il giorno di Natal

6ª

Barbabiettola lo sapete
Serde al bue per ingrassare
Indee noi dobbiamo mangiare
Se non si vuole obbidire

4a

Stoccafisso con merluzzo

Sono Pesci danno a mare

Invece qui dobbiamo mangio il

Tutti g giorni Baccalà

4a

Dried cod and salted cod

They are fish from the sea[1]

Here/now we must eat it

Every day Baccala.[2]

5a

L'arrenga c'he quell pesce

Che mangiano ussai di rado

Invece qui tutto a stufato

Pesce il giorno di Natale.

5a

Herring is the fish

That we rarely eat

Instead, here everything is stewed

Herring is for Christmas Day.[3]

6a

Barbabiettola lo sapete

Serve al bue per ingrassare

Invece noi dobbiamo mangiare

Se non si vuole obudiglia (digiunare)

6a

Red beets/turnips, you know them.

Served to the oxen to get fat

Instead, we must eat them

If you do not want to (starve?)[4]

Author Commentary

1. saltwater fish, probably Norway
2. Dried cod, salted cod, and baccala are all the same thing, prepared in slightly different ways. He was in prison for two years, three months, and three weeks.
3. Herring is a treat for Christmas day, along with Polenta
4. The word obudiglia does not translate. I am guessing it means to starve. There is a verb in modern Italian, digiunare, which means "to fast." The winter of 1916–1917 was known as the "turnip winter." The potato crop in Germany failed. Allies blocked the German ports, there was a labor shortage, and nitrogen used for fertilizer was diverted to be used in explosives. Turnips, usually used to feed livestock, now became a staple food for civilians, soldiers, and prisoners. Tens of thousands died from malnutrition and subsequent diseases. Fedele's daughters, Mafalda and Mary, said that later in life, he refused to eat turnips. They remember him saying that the taste reminded him of when he was forced to eat them from the trash. He never told them he was forced to eat them in prison.

Mauthausen Concentration Camp

THE MAUTHAUSEN CAMP was a concentration/prisoner of war camp not far from the town of Mauthausen in Northwest Austria. The Austrians established the camp in 1914 to hold captured Russian and Serbian soldiers. Those prisoners were forced into labor to build the camp. The structures were hastily constructed wooden barracks, some without doors. A barbed wire fence surrounded the camp. Later in the war, the population at the Mauthausen camp peaked at 80,000 POWS.

TREATMENT

The Italian POWS received the worst treatment. During their first two months of captivity, about 900 of the 11,000 new Italian prisoners died from beatings, hunger, exposure, and disease. This is due in part to the intentional neglect by the Italian government.

୧୷୬

The Italian POWS received the worst treatment. During their first two months of captivity, about 900 of the 11,000 new Italian prisoners died from beatings, hunger, exposure, and disease. This is due in part to the intentional neglect by the Italian government. The consensus opinion of the government was that most of those who surrendered or were captured were cowards or traitors. Therefore, the Italian government intentionally blocked essential relief packages sent by families of the prisoners and from the Red Cross. In the chapter, "The Taking of Black Mountain," Fedele refers to being "Betrayed by my own country." He and his fellow prisoners were dying at the hands of their own leaders. In one diary entry, he writes, "Now we are at the point/*tip of a great boot.*" He believes that his beloved country is figuratively kicking him in the ass and leaving him to die in a concentration camp.

The Italian government was causing starvation. The result was an exceptionally high rate of death. The death rate among Italians in Mauthausen was nine times greater than that of prisoners from other countries. The conditions in the camp were harsh by any standard. The prisoner's diet was almost entirely various types of dried salted fish and beans. By the end of the war, about 100,000 Italians had died in Austrian POW camps.

The Austrians were not above using their captives for propaganda. They had a photography shop in the prison. Fedele and many of the other captives were posed by a professional for these photos. The soldiers were presented as clean-shaven, well-fed, with hair neatly cut, and wearing uniforms in new condition. Their general appearance was that of good health. The reverse side of the photos were postcards. Each prisoner would handwrite the exact same words on the back of the postcard/photo. "Memories of our imprisonment in Austria, greetings and kisses." It is apparent that the Austrians viewed and approved each of these cards before they were mailed to the family back home. The prisoners must have had duplicates that they exchanged among themselves. Fedele gathered and kept nineteen of these postcards. Several of them are addressed, but were not mailed. It is my opinion that these photos were made shortly after they were captured, and before their harsh life as prisoners began. These men had been through months of trench warfare. In the chapter *Homeless Orphan,* he describes their overall condition as poor after living in the trenches for months. Here they are in the photos, looking like new recruits.

Mauthausen was closed at the end of the war. The Nazis reopened it at the beginning of WWII. They used Jewish slave labor to remove the older wooden buildings. With stone from the nearby quarry, the Nazis forced the Jews to construct the stone fortress that became infamous after WWII. Nearly 190,000 Jewish prisoners passed through Mauthausen between 1939 and 1945. About half of them died there. They died from slave labor in the quarry, disease, exhaustion, starvation, beatings, and the gas chamber. Near the end of the war, the camp was liberated by American soldiers. Some of the former prisoners reversed roles with their captors. Many of the German guards did not survive the experience.

Figure 3: Fedele close up from group photo

Figure 4: Group photo of prisoners at Camp Goding, Mauthausen, 1917. Fedele Loria in back row left.

Figure 2: Reverse of group photo. Greetings and kisses, addressed to his mother, Marianna Ferrise.

5°

Ma le Fave son legumi
Che le danno ai cavalli
Ma dei vermi ce ne tanti tanti
Non si possono proprio mangiare,

6°

Cammomilla l'è quell'erba
Che si da per digerire
Invece qui la fan servire
Niente meno che per Te,

7°

Il pane è poi quella cosa
Che è buono da per tutto,
Invece qui è così brutto
Non si può proprio mangiare.

7a

Ma le fave son legumi
Che le danno ai cavalli
Ma dei vermi a me tanti tanti
Non si possono proprio mangiare.

7a

But the fava beans are legumes
That they give to the horses.
But so many worms in the fava beans.
You just cannot eat them.[1]

8a

Cammomilla l'e quell' erba
Che si da per digerire
Invece qui la fan servire
Niente meno che per te.

8a

Chamomile is the herb
That one gives for digestion
Instead, here it feels
It does nothing for you.[2]

9a

Il pane é poi quella cosa
Che e'buono da per tutto
Invece qui e'cosi brutto
Non si può proprio mangier.

9a

The bread is that thing
Which is good everywhere.
But here the bread is very bad.
You just can't eat it.

Author Commentary

1. Fava beans are dried for storage. If they are wet, then they get worms in them. The fava beans were infested with worms.

2. Chamomile is a very common herb that is made into a tea to settle an upset stomach or to stop stomach cramps.

10ª

Vi ripeto cari amici

Il cibo che ci vien dato

Per tanti mesi ci ha annoiato

Un giorno l'arringa l'altro il baccalà

11ª

Io tralascio coi miei versi

Scuse a voi se vi ho annoiato

quante volte ho sognato

La mia bella libertà.

Fine

Sodiny 11/12 917

Fame,

10a

Vi ripeto cari amici

Il cibo che ci vien dato

Per tanti mesi ci la annoinio,

Un giorno l'arringa l'altre il baccalá

11a

Io Tra lascio coi miei versi

Scuse a voi se vi ho annoiato

Quante volte lo sognato

La mia bella libertá

Fine

Goding 11/12/1917

Fame

10a

I repeat to you my dear friends

The food we are given

For so many months we are bored with it.

One day herring, the next day baccala'

11a

I abbreviate my verses.[1]

Excuse me if I have bored you.

How many times, I have dreamed

Of my beautiful liberty.[2]

The end

Goding 11/12/1917

Hunger[3]

Author Commentary

1. I am playing with words/using poetic license in the way I write.
2. This could be a question, but more likely it is a statement.
3. Fedele signs off many of his diary entries with the single word: *Fame* which translates in English to 'Hunger'.

Figure 5: Postcard of prisoner Perro at Goding 2 July 1917.

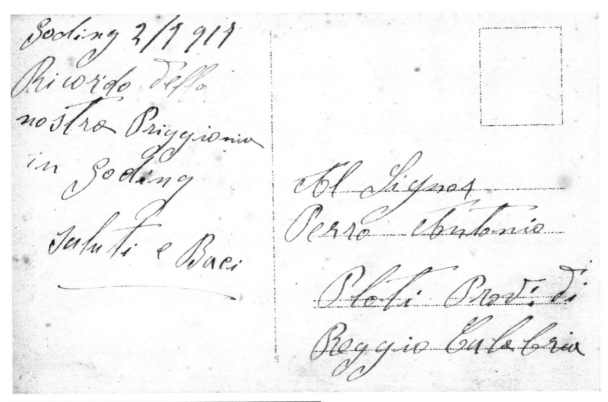

Figure 6: Reverse of postcard Perro

Goding 2/1914
Ricordo della nostra Prigonia Goding,
Saluti and baci

Goding 2/1914
"Memory of our imprisonment in Goding,[2]
Greetings and kisses."

Author Commentary

1. This is one of several unmailed postcards that Fedele exchanged with the other prisoners. In addition to the soldiers' home addresses and family names, all the cards have the same message on the reverse side of the photo.
2. It is interesting to note the similarity between this standard verbiage and the title page of his diary, which is "Memory of my imprisonment in Austria" his signature and date.

Discorso del Prigioniero

1ª

O Italia mia diletta
quante cose ti voglio dire
Abbiamo trovato in Austria
Sol miseria e gran soffrire

2ª

Gente brutta, una faccia scura
Son tenute a comandare
Impiegavan il loro opere
dei malintesi a provocar,

3ª

Il silenzio da noi volevano
Anche quando avevano ragione
Perchè ai ferri o pure al patto
Ci volevano con gran ragione,

22

Discoroso del Prigioniero
"Quante Cose ti Voglio Dire"

Speech of the Prisoner
"Many Things I Want to say to you"

1a

O / tu dice mia dilettá,

Quante cose ti voglio dire[1]

Abiamo trovato in Austria

Sol miseria e gran soffire.

1a

Oh, I say to you my beloved,

Many things I want to say to you.

We have found in Austria

Only misery and great suffering.

2a

Gente brutta con face scure

Son venute a comandare[2]

Impiegavan il loro sapere,[3]

Dei malintosi a provocar.

2a

Evil (mean) people with angry faces.

They came to command.

They used the manner of their ways,

With a lot of malintent to provoke us.

3a

Il silenzio da noi volevano

Anche quando avevamo ragione[4]

Perchè ai ferri o pure al pallo[5]

Ci volevano con gran ragione.[6]

3a

It is our silence that they want.

Even when we were right.

otherwise the iron rod

With good reason they wanted this for us.

Author Commentary

1. He uses the strong form of I want, as if to say I must.
2. to give orders
3. with very bad language and cursing
4. If the prisoners were objecting to the food, conditions, or treatment, they were told to be silent.
5. This sentence does not translate. Perché in this context could mean "otherwise" Ferri refers to a piece of iron. Pallo could be the misspelled word for pole. In this context, and considering the harsh treatment of prisoners, I believe this is a reference to being beaten with an iron rod or a pole for talking back or disobeying an order.
6. With a righteous indignation, they thought we deserved this harsh treatment.

4ª

Una piccola pagnotta in due
di pane nero e disgustoso
Era il cibo più delicato
E per loro il più prezioso.

5ª

La pietanza poi era fatta
Con acqua calda e farina
E formavano degli impasti
Solo adatto per le galline

6ª

Con brodo dei fagioli
Era il cibo che imperava.
Frammischiato con dei cavoli
Farina d'osso oppure di fava

4a

Una piccolo pagnotto in due

Il pane nero e disgustoso

Era il più delicato[1]

E per loro il più prezioso[2]

5a

La pietanza poi era fatto

Con acqua calda e farina

Formavano degli impasti

Solo adatto per le galline[3]

6a

Con brodo dei fagoli

Era il cibo che imperava,

Slammischiato con dei cavoli

Farina d'osso oppure di fava[4]

4a

One small loaf for two.

The black bread is disgusting.

It was the most delicate,

And for them the most precious.

5a

The dish was made

With hot water and flour.

They were making the dough

That was only good for the chickens.

6a

Bean broth

Was the food that prevailed.

(Blended?) together with cabbage.

Bone flour or fava.

Author Commentary

1. As if it was the most delicate
2. They gave out the bread as if it was the most delicate and precious type of food they could give us.
3. Flour and water literally is cheap chicken feed.
4. Ground up animal bones can be used for animal feed. Probably the Austrians mixed some bone flour in the cabbage and fava bean stew.

7ª

La polenta con acqua nera
Di caffè solo in sembianza
Era questo lo stramezzo
Di varietà nella pietanza

8ª

Quando il giorno era di magro
Combinandosi a loro vantaggio
Si ponevano nella gavetta
Del baccalà o del formaggio

9ª

Ma per non troppo annoiarsi
Ogni giorno si cambiava
Trasformando la pietanza
In un sol piatto di sale

7a

La polenta con acqua nera,[1]

Di caffè solo in sembianza.

Era questo la stramezza

Di varietà nella pietanza

8a

Quand il giorno era di magro,[2]

Combinavasi a loro vantaggio.

Ci ponevano nella gavetta

Del baccalà o del formaggio.

9a

Ma per non troppo annoiarvi,

Ogni giorno si cambiava[3]

Strasformando la pietanza

In un sol piato di fave.

7a

Cornmeal with black water,

It was only a semblance of coffee.

It was rubbish

Of the varity of meals.

8a

When the day was skinny

They combined it to their advantage.

They put in the mess tin

Some baccala or some cheese.

9a

But to not bore you too much,

every day they would change,

transforming the dish

into one plate of fava beans.

Author Commentary

1. A bowl of cornmeal and a cup coffee
2. On the days when we ate even less food than normal.
3. The only variety in day-to-day meals lwas between chicken feed dough, salted cod, or bean and cabbage soup.

10°

Le razioni più ridotte
Per non farci indigestione
Ma lo stomaco indegnato
Ne volevano soddisfazione

11°

Fra salute ed aria buona
Fra la fame e allegria
Siam contenti d di aver trovato
Almeno fra essi buona armonia

Fine

Sodingi 12/12 917

Fine

10a

Le razioni più ridotte

Per non farei indigistione

Ma lo stomacho ingegnato¹

Ne volevano sodisfezione

(Volevano che avessimo fame)²

11a

Fra salute ed aria buona

Fra la fame e allegria

Siam contenti di aver trovato

Almeno fra essi buona armonia

Fine

Goding: 12/12/917

Fame³

10a

The rations are smaller

So as not to cause indigestion

But the stomach is angry.

They did not want us to get satisfaction.

(They wanted us to be hungry)

11a

Between health and fresh air,

Between hunger and happiness,

We are happy to have found

At least, between them a good harmony.

The end

Goding: 12/12/917

Hunger⁴

Author Commentary

1. indignant
2. Fedele uses an oblique style of writing. He avoids a graphic description of starvation by using sarcasm to paint the picture. I think he hoped to live long enough that he would be able to take this diary back to Calabria with him. If so, then his mother, sister, and brothers would read it. Perhaps, as he thinks of them, he softens the harsh reality. Later in his diary, he uses the same sarcastic/oblique writing style to describe some of the most horrific battles of WWI. He never gives graphic details of the horrors, death, and destruction that surrounded him.

3. It seems to me that he is pragmatic while putting a positive light on awful circumstances. How can one be hungry and happy at the same time? We can see that he softens the harsh reality of being a prisoner of war. I do believe he is trying to make the best of a very bad situation. His mind, spirit, and body were under great stress, and still, he managed to put ink on paper with a quill pen in a way that few could manage. Most of us would not be able to write such beautiful poetry while starving.

4. I believe Fedele and Ann Frank shared some of the same philosophies. She wrote in her diary, "Where there's hope, there's life. It fills us with fresh courage and makes us strong again. I can shake off everything as I write, my sorrows disappear, my courage is reborn. Work, love, courage, and hope. Make me good and help me cope!"¹

2.0 Anne Frank, The Diary of Anne Frank (London: Longman, 1989).

La presa del Monte nero.

Monte nero dove sei
Traditor della patria mia
Io ho lasciato la casa mia.
Per venirti a conquistare.

2ª

Spunta l'alba il 16 Giugno
Comincia il fuoco d'artiglieria
Il terzo offrini su per la via
Per venirti a conquistar

3ª

Siam arrivati a venti metri
Dal nemico trincerato
E con un assalto entusiasmato
Il nemico fu prigioniero.

La Presa Del Monte Nero
"Taditor Della Patria Mia"

The Taking of Black Mountain
"Betrayed by my own Country"

Monte nero dove sei
Traditor della patria mia[1]
Io ho lasciato la casa mia
Per venirti a conquistare.

2a
Spunta l'alba il 16 Giugno[2]
Comincia il fuoco d'artiglieria
Il terzo alpine su per la via
Per venirti a conquistar

3a
Siam arrivati a venti metri
Dal nemico trimerato
E con un assalto entusiamato
Il nemico fu prigionieri.

Black mountain, where are you?

Betrayed by my own country.

I left my home

To come to you to conquer.

2a

At sunrise on 16 June.

The artillery fire began.

The third alpine (division) is on the way

Coming to conquer you.

3a

We got to within twenty meters

From the entrenched enemy.

And with one enthusiastic assault,

The enemy became prisoners.

Author Commentary

1. Later in the diary, he refers to the politicians and leaders as betraying him and every soldier.
2. The battle of Black Mountain began on the sixteenth of July 1916. This was a fateful day for Fedele, as you will see later in his diary. Several battles were fought around the towns of Gorizia, Tolmino, and Black Mountain in 1915, 1916, and 1917.

4ª

Per venisti a conquistare
Obbiamo perduti molti compagni
Tutti giovanni dai ventuni
E la sua vita non torna piùi

5ª

Quanti pianti quanti sospiri
Che faranno le madre sue.
Anche noi ci può far dei quadri
Se il destin mi a lascià

6ª

Ora mai che i tre cofri
Sventola senza fine colà
Forza al sesto Alpini
Di Tolmino dobbiam andar.

4a

Per venirti a conquistare,

Abbiamo perdii moli compagni

Tutti Giovanni sui ventanni

E la sua vita non torna piú

4a

To come to you to conquer,

We have lost many companions

Every one of them about twenty years old.

And his life will never come back.

5a

Quanti pianti? Quanti sospire,

Che faranno le madre sue

Anche noi si pió far dei quadri,[1]

Le il destin mi a lascia.[2]

5a

How very many tears? So much sobbing.

What will their mothers do?

Even now we can see the painting.

The destiny left to me.

6a

Ora mai che I tre colori[3]

Ventola senza fine colá

Forsa al sesto Alpini[4]

A Tolmino dobbiamo andar.[5]

6a

Now that the three colors

Flies without end.

With the strength of the sixth alpini.

To Tolmino we must go.

Author Commentary

1. We can see the big picture, "the writing on the wall."
2. The destiny that is left to me.
3. The three colors are the Italian flag, green, white, red.
4. The sixth Alpine Regiment
5. The battle at Tolmino Slovenia, began on October 1, 1915.

Ho

E appena quinti saremo

A Tolmino pianteremo la Bandiera

E a Gorizia per Trincea.

a Trieste Vogliamo andar

Fine Soding; il 12/12/91?

Fine;

7a

E appena quinti saremo

A Tolmino pianteremo la bandiera

E a Gorizia per trincea

A Tieste vogliamo andar

Fine Goding 12/12/917

Fame[2]

7a

As soon as we arrive

At Tolmino we will plant the flag.

And to the trenches of Gorizia

To Trieste we must go.[1]

Fine Goding 12/12/917

Hunger

Author Commentary

1. Vogliamo is a very strong desire, almost a command. Gorizia, Tolmino, and Treiste were Slovenian towns occupied by the Germans. He writes, "As soon as we arrive." I assume the intention was to go there, take the towns, and raise the tri-color flag.

2. At the beginning of this chapter, Fedele recalls combat as a soldier. Later, he seems to change his perspective from that of a soldier in combat to that of a prisoner.

3. Situated on Black Mountain was a fortified castle held by the Germans. The position of Black Mountain provided the perfect vantage point for German Artillery. There were several battles for the castle and the surrounding alpine terrain. Fedele mentions Tolmino, which is in the shadow of Black Mountain. This was mountain warfare in the trenches. Tens of thousands of Italians died in battle. Many died from disease, exposure, or in avalanches. Eventually, the Italians won the battle.[1]

2.1   For more details, see Smithsonianmag.com/history/most−treacherous−battle−world−war−1.

La mia Villeggiatura in Trincea.

Al gran Otel Carso 1915 – 1916 Stazione Climata
Bagni luce a gas. asfisianti auto da 305. pronta
tutte le ore alla Stazione.....

Otel Carso.

Antipasti reticolati eletrici con Bocche da lupo.
specialità Doberdò... Minestra con pallottole
dun dun. pesce dirigibile. Sull'isonzo. con Salsa
D'Asburgo"   Piatto Secondo
Arrosto) Bombe di gelatina e fusto....
Aereoplani alla class. con gelatine. esplosivo.
Frutta Negok all'Italiana con Bannana.
di granata; vino l'ambroso di baionetta.
lagrime dei poveri Cristi...

La mia Villeggiatura in Trincea
"Vino l'ambrusco di Baionetta"
Al gran otel Carso 1915–1916[1]

My Vacation in the Trenches
"Lambrusco wine on Bayonets"
The Grand Hotel Carso 1915–1916

Bagno luce a gas asfisianti.	Bathrooms lit with gas that will asphyxiate.
Auto da 305 pronta tutte le ore all stazione . . .[2]	Cars ready 24 hours a day to take you to the station . . .
Otel Carso	Hotel Carso
Antipasti reticolati eletrici, con bocche da lupo.	Appetizer of electric wires with wolves' mouths.
Specialita Doberdo . . .[3]	Specialty of Doberdo . . .
Minestra con pallottole dun dun[4] continued on 38	Vegetable soup with bullets dun dun.

Author Commentary

1. The Carso is not a real hotel. Fedele is using sarcasm to avoid describing the horrors of war in graphic detail. The Carso is a geographical area in Northeast Italy near Venice and Trieste, including parts of Slovenia and Croatia. This mountainous area was the scene of many battles between the Austrians and the Italians. Eventually, the Italians won the war.

2. A bathroom with gas lights would only be found in luxurious accommodations. The phrase "lit with gas" refers to the deadly mustard gas mortars used by the Germans. The auto 305 is a reference to the 305 mm cannons used by both sides. At any time, day or night, you could die by artillery fire. A 305 mm shell will make a crater twenty-five feet deep, and twenty-five feet wide. The shock wave could kill an unprotected person up to one-quarter mile away from the explosion. Perhaps he means a trip to the station is where you get your one-way ticket from hell on earth to Heaven.

3. He is describing the dinner menu from the Hotel Carso. The first course would be an electric wire fence, possibly barbed wire with teeth like a wolf's mouth. Doberdo del lago is a small town in the region of Gorizia near Trieste in the Carso.)

4. The words "dun dun," as he spells it, refer to hollow point bullets. A hollow point bullet will expand on impact. The larger diameter and ragged edge of the expanded bullet make a much larger wound than the traditional pointed full metal jacket bullet. This illegal style of bullet would strike fear into any soldier They were first developed by the English in Calcutta, India, in a town called Dum Dum, with an armory of the same name. In 1898 the Germans had these types of bullets outlawed because they caused excessive and inhumane wounds, thus violating the "Laws of War". This newly outlawed bullet was widely employed by the Germans during WWI.

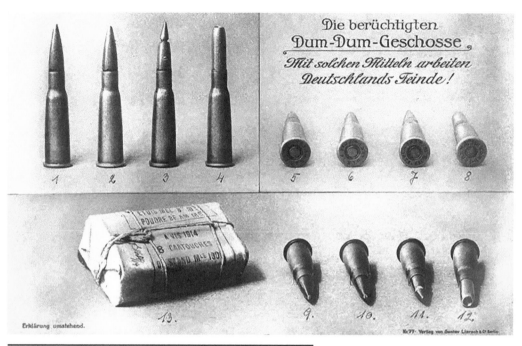

Figure 7: WWI Dum-Dum hollow point bullets

continued from page 37

Pesce dirigibile, sull' Isonzo con salsa D'asburgo.[1]	Fish from an airship on the Isonzo river with salsa in the style of D'asburgo.
Piatto Secondo	Second Course
Arrosta Bombe di gelatina e gusto . . .	Roasted bombs in gelatin is good
Aeroplani alla class Con gelatine esplosiva.	Airplane a la carte with explosive gelatin.
Frutta nespole alll'Italiana con Bannana granatai.	Nespole fruit in the Italian style with banana grenades.
Vino l'ambrusco di baionetta[2]	Lambrusco wine from bayonets.
Lagrime dei poveri Christi . . . [3]	Tears of the poor Christi.[4]

Author Commentary

1. Fish from an airship might refer to bombs dropped from an airship. The Isonzo river was the dividing line between the two armies. There were twelve major battles fought along this river. This theater of war was referred to as the battle of the Isonzo.
2. Lambrusco is a type of sparkling red wine.
3. Aldo's interpretation of this phrase is this: Fedele is referring to all the unfortunate soldiers who have been unjustly thrust into this war and are being punished to the point of death, through no fault of their own.
4. Daniella's interpretation is that he is referring to the soldiers as "poor devils, or poor fellows" who are forced to endure this punishment. The word "dei" is used as a plural for these or those or all of those. I am inclined to agree with Daniella's view; however, either could be correct.

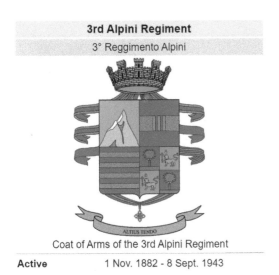

3rd Alpini Regiment

3° Reggimento Alpini

Coat of Arms of the 3rd Alpini Regiment

| Active | 1 Nov. 1882 - 8 Sept. 1943 |

Figure 8: Coat of Arms 3rd Alpini Regiment. In the poem "The Taking of Black Mountain," Fedele indicates that he is in the 3rd alpine regiment.

Figure 9: Anonoymous soldier in uniform

Fedele would recognize this hat immediately. This distinctive hat was standard issue for those light infantry troops assigned to mountain warfare. He was assigned to one of the alpine regiments. The alpine trooper hat is also known as the Cappello Alpino.

Figure 10: Alpine regimental hat with feather

The black raven feather was worn on the left when not in a combat zone, and on the right of the helmet during combat. The alpine regiments were proud to carry their nickname, "the black feathers," or in Italian, "Le Penne Nere."

Figure 11: Alpine helmet

This helmet bears the emblem of an Alpine regiment. It was the standard issue, and Fedele would have worn this helmet or one very much like it. This style of helmet, known as the Adrian helmet, was designed in 1915 by the French army general Luis Adrian. A helmet became necessary equipment because soldiers in the trenches were being wounded by shrapnel from overhead artillery explosions. This style of head protection was quickly adopted by all the armies in WWI. The helmets were not effective against bullets, but they significantly reduced the number of shrapnel wounds.

Figure 12: Soldiers climbing cliff. Italian Soldiers scale Monte Nero on the Karst plateau during the second battle of the Isonzo, 1915. Note the trademark black raven feather in the caps of the soldiers of the Alpini regiments.

Figure 13: Officer with soldiers

Figure 14: 105 mm cannon

Figure 15: Italian soldiers with 305 cannon

Figure 16: 305 mm cannon shells

Figure 17: 305 mm shell created this crater

Figure 18: Fortress siege gun

Figure 19: Skeletal remains of Italian soldiers at Gorizia

12 Battles of Isonzo—The War in the Mountains

THE 12 BATTLES along the Isonzo river were among the most extreme battlefields in history. Nothing like it has been seen before or since in the history of warfare.

More than one million Austrians, Hungarians, and Italians perished along the 400-mile-long theatre of war. I could write several pages on the subject. If you want to know more than this brief accounting, then you will want to watch these two YouTube videos. *The Most Insane Battlefield in History: World War One in the Alps* will set the scene for you in four minutes and nineteen seconds. The other video, *WWI Secrets Hidden in Slovenian Mountains—Isonzo: The war in the mountains*, is forty-five minutes long. This in-depth documentary brings to life many of the specific places and events that Fedele mentions in his writing. These videos put living color onto the pages he wrote in black and white. They will let you see the places where he fought and give you a better understanding of what he witnessed as history was being made. I highly recommend that you watch both videos.

The Karst plateau, when translated to Italian, is "the Carso." Fedele makes several references to Carso "Hotel" Carso, Gorizia, and Trieste. We cannot be sure of how many of the twelve battles around the Isonzo river that he took part in. We can say with certainty that he was there.

Fedele wrote that the Battle of Black Mountain began at sunrise on June 16, 1916. His last day of combat was July 6, 1916. Perhaps his memory was off by a month or so. On that fateful day, he received two wounds in the abdomen and possibly one in the back. Evidence of these wounds indicated he was likely hit by shrapnel and knocked unconscious from the shock wave of an artillery shell explosion. Fedele never talked about his wartime experiences, so we don't have all the details. His daughters were surprised to learn that he was a combat-wounded veteran. We learned of his wounds, the surgery, and his recovery from an extraordinarily rare hospital chart that was preserved along with his diary. Across the top of his two-page medical chart are these words: "Questionnaire About Abdominal Injuries."

Questionnaire About Abdominal Injuries

AN AUSTRIAN DOCTOR and at least one nurse created this handwritten medical chart. At that time, they did not have photocopies. This two-page document would have been copied by hand from a standard form that outlines the protocol of care for patients with abdominal wounds. This chart has the handwriting of at least two people. Most of the writing copied from the standard form was probably written by a nurse or an aide with neat handwriting. Although the document has faded a bit in one hundred and six years, you can see that the doctor's handwriting in pencil is not as neat but still precise. There are many details about his treatment and condition. For example, Fedele Loria of the 133rd regiment, 11th company ate at 11:55 (pm) the evening before he was wounded. He was found unconscious at 11:00 am on July 6, 1916. Five hours later, he was questioned to complete this document. The Germans and Austrians are well known for precision and good record keeping. It is incredible that in a combat zone field hospital, such a record would even be written, much less given to a prisoner. The fact that Fedele obtained and kept this document is remarkable.

The war ended approximately twenty-eight months later, in November 1918. Many of the former

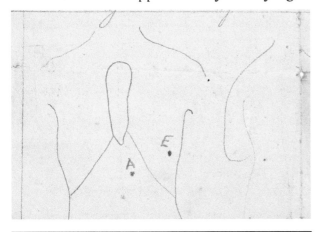
Figure 20: Detail of drawing of abdominal wounds

prisoners had been weakened by malnutrition and diseases. Now they faced an arduous journey over the alps to Army bases in northern Italy. Some traveled by train or cart, others walked up to 150 miles to the nearest base, where they were expecting to be discharged and to go home soon. The military and political establishments were decidedly negative towards those who were captured. They were interred for months and were subject to interrogation and trials to demonstrate that they were not traitors and that they did not surrender in a cowardly manner. The number of Italian prisoners exceeded 250,000. It would take many months to interrogate or prosecute so many soldiers. Fedele was among those who were held for more than a year after the armistice was signed. We don't know to what extent he was interrogated regarding the circumstances of his capture. We do know that he had the "Questionnaire of Abdominal Wounds" with him. This document is irrefutable proof that he did not surrender in a cowardly or traitorous manner. He was rendered unconscious, probably by the concussion of an artillery shell, wounded in at least two places, and promptly taken prisoner.

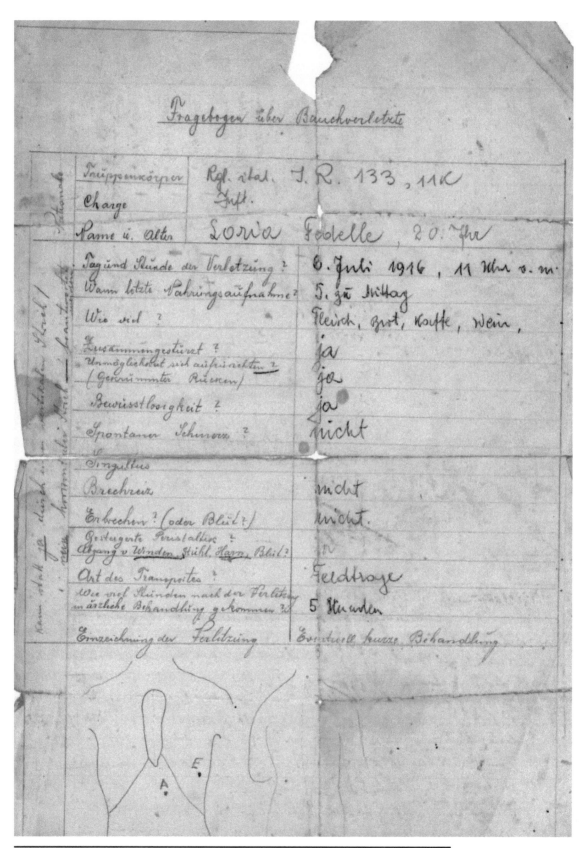

Figure 21: German Questionnaire of Abdominal Wounds, pg 1

Questionnaire of Abdominal Wounds		
Origin	Troop Body	Italian Regiment I.R. 133, 11 C
	Rank	Infantry
	Name and age	Loria Fedele age 20
Can be answered with a vertical stroke for yes/ or a horizontal stroke for no —	Day and time of injury	6 July 1916, 11:00 a.m.
	When was the last time you ate?	11:55
	How much?	Meat, bread, coffee, wine
	Collapsed?	yes
	Curved back (fetal position)	yes
	Unconscious?	yes
	Spontaneous pain?	yes
	Hiccups	
	Nausea	no
	Throwing up? (or blood?)	no
	Intestinal peristalsis Release of gas, stool, urine, blood?	yes
	How was he transported?	stretcher
	How long since the injury before he was examined by a doctor?	5 hours
	Labeling of the injury	Probability short treatments

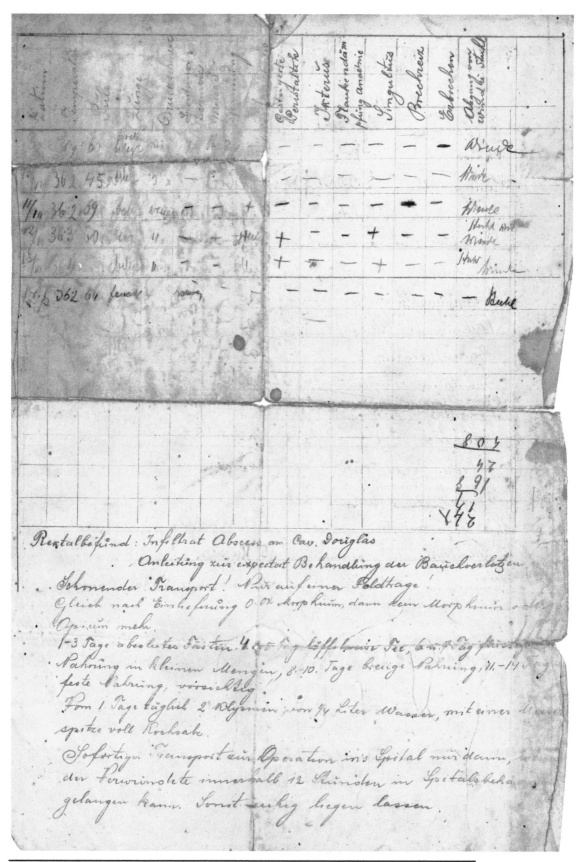

Figure 22: German Questionnaire of Abdominal Wounds, pg 2

Date	Temperature	Pulse	Lungs	Back Pain	Spontaneous Pain	Muscle Tone	S–t—io??	Gastric Peristalsis	Jaundice	Abdominal auscultation	singultus	Vomiting	Gas/Stool
9/	36.9	60	dry coated	little	yes	?	—	—	—	—	—	—	?
10/7	36.2	45	coated	little	—	—	—	—	—	—	—	—	gas
11/3	36.2	69	wet	//	—	—	+	—	—	—	—	—	gas
12/	36.3	60	wet	//	—	—	little	+	—	—	+	—	gas/ stool
13/7	36.4	?	coated coated coated	//	—	—	little	+	—	—	+	—	stool/ gas
14/	36.2	64	moist	//	little	—	—	—	—	—	+	—	stool

Report Findings: Infiltrate and Abscess Cav?? Douglas??
Instructions for expected handling of abdominal injuries
Gentle transport! On a stretcher!
Directly after admission administer 0.02 mg of morphine then no more morphine or opium.
Days 1–3 absolute fasting. Days 4–5 spoons full of tea. Days 6–7 liquid diet
in small amounts. Days 8–19 porridge (baby food diet). 11–14
regular diet, carefully.
Daily from the first day ?? drink ¼ liter of water with
one knife point of salt.
Transport as soon as possible to the operating room.
To the hospital within 12 hours for surgery.
Otherwise let him lay quietly.

Details of the chart

THE DATE PROBABLY refers to the number of days post-injury. For example, 11/3 indicates eleven days/examined at three o'clock.

Temperature is in degrees centigrade. 36.2° equals 97° Fahrenheit. This normal temperature means that he did not have a fever, or an infection.

Gastric peristalsis refers to the involuntary and rhythmic movement of muscles of the intestines. No bowel movement with little or no gas would be normal for a few days following anesthesia.

Wound drainage is negative, which is another indication that he did not have an infection.

"Otherwise let him lay quietly." Some assumptions could be made here. Hospitals and surgeons will, by necessity, treat the most seriously wounded first. The exact nature or details of his injury are not in the chart. Given that his surgery was nine days after his injury, then I assume his wounds were not life-threatening. These post-operative instructions are standard and would be appropriate for the repair of a perforated bowel or abdominal injury. Wound "A" is at the level of the stomach. There is no infection present, so it is unlikely he had bowel surgery. He has a serious but not life-threatening injury. Wound "E" is above the diaphragm. Again, we can only guess at the severity. There is a drawing of the posterior torso with a "dot" indicating a wound. The first words of the report reference an abscess. It would not be unusual to have a minor sore or even a boil after living in the trenches.

I have made several assumptions about his wounds and treatment. There are so many unanswered questions. If only we could ask him about this episode of his life. One thing is certain. This questionnaire is not just a historical document. It is a treasured family heirloom with a value that cannot be measured.

Italy Choses Sides

Italy had been an ally of the Austro-Hungarian Empire until April 1915, when Italy signed a secret treaty with the United Kingdom. In May 1915, Italy declared war on Austria, and by June, the Italian army was poised to attack. Troops massed along the Isonzo River, which defined the border between Italy and Austria in 1915. Called the Soča River by the Austrians, it wound through the incredibly rough and mountainous terrain of the Julian Alps. It was perhaps the worst terrain a soldier could imagine to wage an assault.

Figure 23: 305 mm Austro Hungarian cannon

The Italian commanding general, Luigi Cadorna, vastly underestimated the effectiveness of machine guns and was convinced that attacking with a frontal assault was the best strategy for success. That meant charging his troops directly toward the enemy's strong points in the hope of overcoming the enemy's forces through attrition. However, the Austrians were well prepared for battle with an extensive array of well-emplaced heavy artillery all along the mountain ridges and fortified machine guns, which were effectively positioned to defend every possible avenue of advance. Despite the fact that the Italians enjoyed a three-to-one superiority in terms of the number of troops, the disastrous tactics used by their leader resulted in abysmal progress on the battlefield. Under intense fire from the Austrians and in horribly mountainous terrain, which significantly restricted their ability to maneuver, the Italians found it nearly impossible to gain any ground. After six weeks of minimal success with heavy Italian casualties, Cadorna was compelled to order a pause to his attack and regrouped his forces. But after only two weeks of rest, the Italians launched another poorly planned assault.

Fedele was serving in the 3rd Alpine Regiment, which was positioned on the northern end of the campaign near the town of Tolmin. As the Italians advanced, they depended upon pack horses for all their supplies. Without mountain roads or even footpaths, the transport and use of heavy artillery was totally impractical. As the battle progressed, the harsh mountainous terrain made it increasingly

Figure 24: Italians hauling heavy artillery over rough terrain in the Carso. 18 July 1915, Isonzo

more challenging to supply the Italians at the front of the battle with even the most basic supplies, such as food and ammunition.

Despite the efforts of their professional officer corps, morale among the troops plummeted. They had lost all confidence in their commanding officers as well as the leadership back in Rome. This lack of confidence was, in part, fueled by this statement made by Benito Mussolini, who said, "This Italy is at the front of the war with our heart and soul. If need be, the first human wall will be followed tomorrow by a second, then by a third. Our goal is victory irrespective of the cost." This attitude expressed in that statement of Mussolini's and the statements of others among the general staff were, in part, why he wrote "Betrayed by my own country" in "The Taking of Black Mountain."

During the sixth battle of the Isonzo, in July and August 1916, the towns of Mt. Saint Busi, Santa Maria, and Santa Lucia were captured by the Italians. Fedele made several references to these towns and other surrounding locations. It is likely that he was injured and captured during the beginning of this campaign.

Sixteen months after he became a prisoner, the Italians were soundly defeated in the 12th battle of Isonzo at Caporetto on November 19, 1917. The fighting in that battle cost the Italians 10,000 killed, 20,000 wounded, and 250,000 captured. The retreat before surrender was twenty-five kilometers. During this offensive, the Austrians used poison gas, heavy artillery, high explosives, and flame throwers. At the end of the day, Italian morale was so low that many willingly surrendered. Officials of the Italian government suspected cowardice, treason, and collusion with the enemy because the collapse of the army was so widespread. For these reasons, the Italian government blocked aid packages from the soldiers' families and from the Red Cross during much of the war. Tens of thousands of Italians suffered or died unnecessarily as a result.

Figure 25: Italian staff officers during the Isonzo Campaign

Figure 26: Isonzo campaign 18 July 1915

AUTHOR'S NOTE

His diary covers a time span of only five and a half months of what was a much longer time in captivity. Why did he not write during the entire time? We can only guess at the possible answers. Perhaps he did not have any more ink or paper. Maybe he was forbidden to write anymore. Could it be that this diary is one in a series, and only this one survived? Who knows? Much is lost to time, so many things we will never know.

Figure 27: Hundreds of Italians captured at Caporetto

Figure 28: Five German soldiers escorting 20 captured Italians after the battle of Caporetto

Varietà

ore 14 gare d'aviazione internazionale con tiri a volo.

ore 15 Concerto musicale e ciclo... Prenderanno parte i seguenti istrumenti... Flauto modello 1891.

Clarino da 90... Cornetta da 95 Corni da 105.

Bombardino da 149 Contrabasso da 209 Bassi da 270

Gran cassa da 305...

Il rancio dei soldati al fronte 1ª Pallottola al burro con relativo fischio. 2ª Brodo con punta penetrante. 3ª Maccheroni a proiettoli della rinomata casa gruppi...

4ª Bistecche alla shrapnel con sorpresa

5ª Contorno con bombe d'aeroplani a gas asfissianti...

6ª Frutta, granate, e nespole.

7ª Vino Rosso del sangue umano...

8ª Bottiglia ormai stravecchia del 305 o 420.

Varietà

"Da Vazione internazionale con Tiri a Volo"[1]

Variety

"An invitation to International Skeet Shooting/Target Practice"

Ore 14 gare da vazione internazionale con tiri a volo[2]

At 14:00 a session of international invitation to shoot skeet.

Ore 15 concerto musicale ecosè . . .

At 15:00 the musical concert will be like this . . .

Prenderanno parte i Sequenti strumenti . . . Flauto modello 1891

the following instruments will take part . . . Flute model 1891

Clarino da 70. Cornetta da 75 Corni da 105

70 Clarinet. 75 Coronet 105 Horns

Bombardino da 169 Contrabasso dal 209 Bassi da 270 Bombardino 169 mm

Bombardino 169 mm Contrabass drum 209 mm Bass drum 270 mm

gran cassa da 305 . . .[3]

Grand bass drum 305 mm . . .

Author Commentary

1. In Italian, Varietà refers to an evening of dining and entertainment. He could be referring to a famous dinner theatre in Venice known as Cinema Varietà.
2. 14:00=2:00 pm The moving targets would be the soldiers on both sides.
3. Every one of these "instruments" refers to the size of a cannon and its caliber in millimeters. Except for Flauto 1891, which refers to the model 1891 Carcano Rifle, the standard issue rifle for Italian infantry in WWI and WWII. It was referred to as "Novantuno," which is Italian for ninety-one. Fedele would have used this rifle in combat.

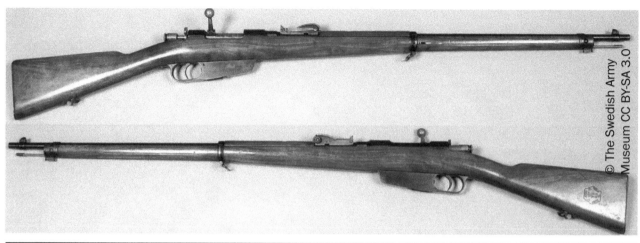

© The Swedish Army Museum CC BY-SA 3.0

Figure 29: Italian Model 1891 Carcano Rifle

Il Rancio dei Soldati al fronte	The Rations of the soldiers at the front.

Il Rancio dei Soldati al fronte

"Servia dalle Signorine Mitragliatrici"[1]

1a *Pallottola al burro con relative fischio . . .*

2a *Brodo con punta penetrante[2]*

3a *Maccheroni a proiettoli della rinomata casa gruppi*

4a *Bistecche alla srappnel con sorpersa*

5a *Contorno con bombe d'arreoplani a gas asfisianti*

6a *Frutta granate e nespole.[3]*

7a *Vino rosso del sangue umano.*

8a *Bottiglia ormai stovecchia del 305 al 420*

The Rations of the soldiers at the front.

"Served by the Machine Gun Ladies"

1a Bullets in butter with the sound of whistling or ricocheting bullets . . .

2a Broth with penetrating tips.

3a Macaroni projectiles from the renowned house of gruppi

4a Shrapnel steak with a surprise.

5a Side dish of bombs with asphyxiating gas from airplanes.
6a Medlar fruit Grenades.

7a Red wine from human blood.

8a A very old worn—out bottle of the 305 to the 420.

Author Commentary

1. On Italian menus the courses are numbered in this manner, 1a, 2a, etc.
2. We cannot be 100% sure that Fedele is referring to flechettes, but it is likely. Flechettes were low-tech arrows about eight inches long, with stability fins that would be dropped from an Austrian airplane. The plane would have boxes full of flechettes, the pilot would pull a release cord and drop hundreds of aerodynamic steel arrows on the soldiers in the trenches. First invented by the Italians, they were silent and deadly. A flechette could penetrate helmets and bones. Later in the war, the use of flechttes was adopted for use by all sides.
3. Medlar is a fruit about the size of a hand grenade
4. Different size cannon shells used by both armies

Unmailed postcard of prisoner addressed to Africa at Goding 28 May 1917.

"Memory of our imprisonment in Goding 28 May 1917. Greetings."

Figure 30: Postcard of prisoner addressed to Africa

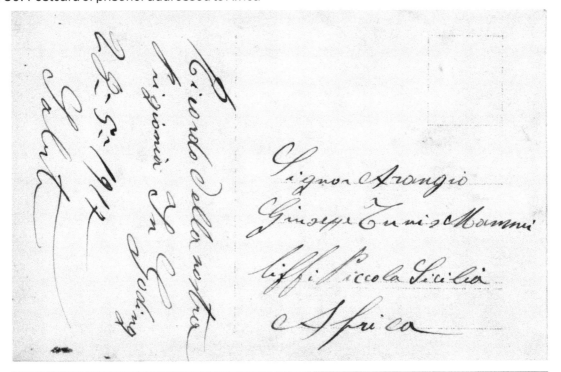

Figure 31: Reverse of unmailed postcard of prisoner addressed to Africa.

Il pranzo è assai saporito ma anche indigesto

10ª Il pranzo e servita dalle signorine mitragliatrici in modo inaccettabile. 11ª Se qualcuno volesse prendere parte a questo invito venga pure da Santa Maria e Santa Lucia, ed a Tolmino sicuro.

Che perde l'appetito.

12ª I fumatori della società affamata dichiarano otto ore di lavoro tutte le notti

13ª Il miglior rancio dei soldati è il riso con quattro ore di cottura al fuoco, e cinque di marmitta, e così si può gridare evviva la Guerra

14ª Datemi una risposta o farabutti interventisti se avete la Coscienza...

La salute del soldato al fronte.

Grande diarea su e giù per la Trincea la volta che ci s'andava in ricognizione

Ci tocca sedere giù

La Salute del Soldato al Fronte
"Per Riposami un Minute Devo Nascondermi un Buco"

The Health of the Soldier at the Front
"To Rest for a Minute, I Must Hide in a Hole"

Grand diarea su e giu per la trimecea.

Much diarrhea up and down the trenches.

La volta ch ci d'andar su di corsa,

The time we must go in a hurry,

Ci tocca sedere giù.

We must sit down.

Il pranzo è assai saporito ma anche indigesto

The lunch is so flavorful, but indigestible.

10a Il pranzo e servita dalle signorine mitragliatrici in modo in aspettabile

10a The lunch is served by the machine gun ladies in the expected way.

11a Se qualcuno volesse prendere parte a questo invito venga pure a Santa Maria e Santa Lucia ed a Tolmino sicuro che perde l'appettitio.[1]

11a If someone wants to take part in this invitation come to Santa Maria and Santa Lucia and to Tolmino. I am sure you would lose your appetite.

12a I fumatori della società affamata dichiarono otto ore di lavoro tutte le notti.[2]

12a The smokers of the starved soci— ety have declared eight hours of work every night.

13a Il miglior rancio dei soldatei è il riso con quattro ore di sottura al fuoco, e cinque di marmitta, e cose si può gridare ed viva la Guerra

13a The best ration for the soldiers is rice with four hours on the fire, and five hours in the pot. Then if you want to, shout, long live the war.

14a Datemi una risposta o fara t interventisti se aveti la coscienza[3]

14a Give me an answer, or it will be for everyone to intervene if you have a conscience.

Author Commentary

1. Tolmino, Santa Maria, and Santa Lucia are towns that were locations of battles in Austria and Italy.
2. The smoker/fumatori is a flame thrower. This weapon was used by the Austrians during the battle of Caporetto.
3. Datami is a demand, not a request.

Si corre subito alla visita Medica accennando mal
di testa e mi caccia fuori come una Bestia se in vece
e mal di corpo, mi tratta come porco; se poi
accennando mal di petto, mi perdono il rispetto, se i
piedi son gelati mi mandano di Corde, ai reticolati
se mi sento male ai denti mi fanno lavorar, nei
Camminamenti, se la febbre e ai 39 mi mandano di piccol
posto, mangiando rancio troppo riscappato, divento
ammalato, all'ora per guarigione mi mandano
d'isplorazione. Per riposarmi un minuto deve
nascondermi in un buco, altrimenti per medicina e'e
Trincea sera e mattina ....

In conclusione del nostro dire bisogna star qui
a soffrire, ma almeno e'una contentezza a
a uccidere pidocchi quando sono di dedetta.
Quando non ò altro da fare continuo queste bestie
adammazzare, ci vuole altro cari Signori, a
riasciugare questi dolori; ci vuol della.

Author Commentary

1. I think he means to cure a headache. The caffeine in chocolate can sometimes cure a headache.

Li corre subito all visita medica accenuando mal di testa	He runs immediately to the doctor if he signs of a severe headache,
È mi caccia fuori come una bestia. Se invece è mal di corpo, mi tratta come porosi	He chases me out like a beast. If my body hurts, he treats me like a pig.
Accennando mal di petto me perdono il rispetto. Se i piedi son gelato mi mandono di corve ai reticolati	Hinting of chest pain, I am losing their respect. If my feet are frozen, they send me to patrol the barbed wire.
Se mi sento male ai denti mi fanno lavore nei caminamenti.	If I have a tooth ache, they make me work in the walkways (the trenches)
Se fa febbre e ai 38 mi mandono di piccolo posto mangiando ranco troppo sciappato divento ammalato	If I have a fever of 100°F. they send me to a place to eat rations that are too wet and soft I get sicker.
all'ora per guarigioni mi mandano displorazione . . .	Now to get better they send me on reconnaissance . . .
Per riposami un minute devo nascondermi un buco	To rest for a minute, I must hide myself in a hole.
Altrimenti per medicina è trimcea sera e mattina . . .	Otherwise for medicine, it is the trenches evening and morning . . .
In conclusione del nostro dire bisogna star qui a soffrire,	In conclusion of our need to tell, we must stay here to suffer,
ma almeno è una contentezza a uccidere pidocchi quando sono di vedettai;	but at least it is a happiness to kill lice/ fleas when I am on guard duty.
Quando non o' altro da fare continuo queste bestie a da mazzare,	When there is nothing else to do I con— tinue to smash those fleas/lice.
Ci vuole altro curi Signori a ricupperare questi dolori;	Sirs, we need something else to recover from these pains.
Ci vuol della cioccolata per far venire la testa ammalata[1]	We need some of chocolate to make a headache
Se per caso mi incanto un poco mi legano al'avani alla trimcea in mezzo al fuoco.	If by chance I am (distracted/ daydream— ing) they put me at the front trench in the middle of (enemy) fire.
Il 18 marzo stavo bene, la landra nella sua casa bianca[2]	The eighteenth of March (1916) I was fine. The courtesan/vegetable in her white house.

2. Depending on your choice of the two definitions for "La landra," he was either, eating a vegetable called landra in a white house, or he spent the day with a courtesan in her white house. This sentence about the eighteenth of March seems completely out of place, unless you are willing to consider that it may be linked to the thoughts in the previous sentence about daydreaming.

Cioccolata per far venire la testa ammalata.

Se per caso mi incanto un poco mi legano d'avanti alla trincea in mezzo al fuoco.

Il 18 Marzo stavo bene. Salandra nella sua casa Bianca.

Caro Amico

Nella ricorrenza del mio onomastico mi sento in dovere d'invitarti alla festa che verrà data con tutto il mio buon cuore certo non vorrai mancare al mio invito dunque ti mando il seguente Menu? Antipasto Srapnel alla Viennese Pranzo granate da 305 in esplosiva alla Trentina, granate da 151 con grande volo e odore di gas asfissianti, Bombe incendiarie specialità di Lubiana.

Paramples da 105 alla monfalcone, formaggio gelatina all'inglese. Frutta mele di granate di tutte le qualità... Dolci piccoli...

Author Commentary

1. The Catholic Church designates feast days to celebrate and honor the memory of important saints. If you are named after one of the saints, then this would be like

Caro Amico

"Certo con Vorrai Mancare al mio Invitio"

Dear Friend

"I am Sure you Will not Want to Miss my Invitation"

Nella ricorrenza del mil onomastico mi sento in dovere d'invitarti all festa che verrà data con tutto il mio buon cuore[1]

certo non vorrai mancare al mio invitio

dunque ti mando il sequente menu?

Antipasto Srappnel alla Viennese

Pranzo granate da 305[2] in

esplosiva all Trientina, Granate

Dal 151[2] con grande volo e odore di gas asfisianti,

Bombe incendiarie specialità di Lubiania.[3]

Paraples da 105[2] alla Monfalcone[5], Formagio gelatina all'inglese.[4]

Frutta mele di granate di tutte le qualità . . . dolci piccolo,

On the anniversary of my name day I feel compelled to invite you to the party that will be given with all my good heart

certainly you will not want to miss my invitation,

therefore, I am sending you the following menu?

Antipasto Shrapnel in the Vienna style

Lunch of grenades from the 305

Grenade explosives in the style of Trento,

From the 151 a great flight and odor of asphyxiating gas,

Incendiary bombs specialty of Lubiania.

Paraples From the 105 in the style of Monfalcone, Gelatin cheese in the English style.

Apple fruit grenades of every quality . . . little sweet deserts.

having two birthday parties per year. On this day, it is customary to take the day off work, prepare a lot of food, and invite all your friends to celebrate with you.

2. mm cannon
3. Slovenia
4. A type of cheese from Trento, Italy
5. Austria

Cannoncini di cioccolata, con sorpresa e confetti esplosivi: Novità della casa. ... ... Caffè alla Gorizia. Avvertenza 37. La festa verrà rallegrata dalla meglio suono diritto, dall'abilissima signorina Mitragliatrice. La marsina seguirà un scelto programma composto di graziose suonate tra le quali la danza dei feriti e la sinfonia dei morti del maestro Terrore. Durante la notte splendida illuminazione, dissimile bengala dartaggi all'unisoni non potranno intervenire che persone e riunite. Del detto piastrino di riconoscimento è stato dato a loro una maschera antitifica con un paio occhiali per salvarsi dall'esplosione di qualche tubo o da eventuali incidenti.

Verranno messi fili di reticolati in torno all'albergo e è severamente proibito oltre passare la linea senza. L'autorizzazione del sotto scritto.

***

Author Commentary

1. Confetti is not the colored paper used here in America during parades or celebrations. In this sense, he is probably referring to flying shrapnel as the surprise. Confetti are brightly colored chocolate-covered almonds. My family and I were honored guests for a dinner party at the home of one of our cousins in San Giovanni in Fiore. Our tour guide/translator, Antonella, suggested we bring a certain type of gift basket to our

Cannoncini di cioccolata con sorpresa e confetti esplosivi

from little cannons chocolate with explosive surprises and confetti.

Novità dalla casa (dei proiettili a punta cava)

Novità della casa dum dum²...

News from the house (of hollow point bullets)
News from the house of dum dum...

Caffè alla Gorizia

Coffee in the style of Gorizia.

Divertenza 37³

Entertainment 37

La festa verrra rallegrata dal meglio suono diritto d'alla bilissima signorina Mitragliatrice,

The party would surely be better with the beautiful sounds of the lady machine gunners.

La marcia seguira un scelto programma composta di graziose suonate

The march will follow a choice program composed of the gracious sounds (tunes)

Tra le quali la danza dei feriti e la sinfonia dei morti

Including the dance of the wounded, and the symphony of the dead.

Del maestro terrore ... Durante la notte spledita ill'uminazione

From the maestro of terror. During the night's shining illuminations,

Disimile bengale da raggi l'uminosi non potranno intervenire

like fireworks/the rays of the sun, they are not able to intervene

Che persone reunite del detto piastrino Di riconscimento

That gathering of people that wear breastplate (rank) of an officer

è sarà dato a loro una Maschera antitifica con un pai d'occhiali per salvarsi d'all esplusione di qualche tubo o da ventuali incidenti;

to them will be given a gas mask and a pair of safety glasses to save oneself from an explosion of a tube of chlorine gas, or an unfortunate accident.

Verranno messi fili direticolati in torno all'albergo ed de severamente proibito oltre passare la linea senza l'authorizazione del sotto scritto.⁴

Barbed wire was placed all around the hotel, and it is strictly prohibited to cross the line without my authorized signature.

hostess as this is a long-standing tradition in Calabria. At the local flower shop, the florist knew exactly what Antonella wanted. She prepared a lovely basket of flowers, along with a few trinket items, and colored confetti lining the bottom of the basket, and all wrapped up in colored paper and tied with ribbons. Our hostess, Maria Teresa Marra, immediately recognized the gift that we had for her. She sincerely appreciated it, and we were very warmly welcomed into her home.

2. The name of the town in India where hollow point bullets were invented.

3. refers to the 37 mm cannon

4. "sotto scrito" literally means "my signature." A signature would have been needed to allow someone to pass through the lines.

Figure 32: Mustard gas attack

Author Commentary

Mustard gas is a colorless, odorless, heavier than air gas. The enemy would wait for daylight and favorable winds to launch the gas tubes. Incoming artillery shells contained glass tubes. The glass would break on impact allowing the liquid form of the gas to evaporate and then spread. This would have a tremendous psychological effect; sickening fear would spread among the infantry. When the trenches filled with gas, the soldiers had to choose injury or death by gas, or exit the trenches to face enemy machine gun fire. Symptoms would appear the day after exposure. They include skin burns, painful blisters that ooze yellow fluid, severe eye irritation, uncontrolled tearing, temporary blindness, and extreme respiratory difficulties. The gas was very reactive with moisture on the skin. The blisters would be concentrated in moist areas of the body, such as the arm pits and groin. The gas killed only 2–3 percent of those exposed. Often, long periods of hospitalization would be required to recover. Those that were exposed to mustard gas and survived were at higher risk of developing cancers later in life. In his diary, he did not specifically say that he was or was not exposed. We know he was either near or in the battles where the gas was used. Fedele died at age seventy-seven. He lived for fifty-five years after the war ended. His cause of death was abdominal cancer. Did mustard gas contribute to his death? We will never know.

Figure 33: Mussolini as an Italian soldier, 1917

1. Interventionists refers to those who are politicians or decision makers. Benito Mussolini was a leading spokesperson for Fasci di azione rivoluzionaria. He was very much in favor of interfering and getting into the war in the name of the democratic/revolutionary political party.

Gli interventisti d'Italia, l'anno dichiarato e' racchiusero nel dolore la popolazione.... Avete ragione voi benpensate in vostra coscienza ma il vostro cuore dibatte forte abbastanza. Ditemi un po gridavate avanti ed invece noi siete rimasti a casa perché lungi dai colpi e dai confetti non si teme di morire.. Voi andavate dicendo ai poveri soldati viva la guerra. Armiamoci e partite voi che siete coraggiosi usando alla morte. Qui sono i campi sanguinosi dove la baionetta affronta attacchi scacciando il nemico.... Fatevi avanti o vili o falsi se credete di aver un cuore sincero mentre si occupava il monte nero voi dormivate sui letti bianchi e in conclusione rinnegate con mente riscaldata di zampogne chiusi? Chi vostri comuni non

Gli interventisti d'Italia l'anno
"Fine te la una Volta o Disgraziati"

The Year of the Interventionalists of Italy
"End it Once and for all, you Disgraced People"[1]

dichiarato è racchiusero nel dolore la popolazione ne . . . Avete ragione

(The inteventionalists) told the people we feel your pain . . . You are right

Noi compensavate in nostra coscienza ma il vosto cuore vi batte forte abbastanza.[1]

We are compensated in our conscience but your hearts beat with strength.

Ditmi un po gridavate avanti ed invecce poi sieti

You shout at me to go forward and instead

Rimasti a casa perchè lungi dai colpi e dai confetti non si teme di morire,

You stay at home therefore far from the blows and confetti, you are not afraid to die.

Voi andate dicendo ai poveri Soldati, viva la Guerra

All of you were going around saying to the poor soldiers, Long live the war.

Armiamoci e partite voi che siete corragiosi usando all a morte,

Let's arm ourselves and depart all you who are courageous (going) to death.

Qui sono i campi sanguinoso dove la baionetta affronta attacchi scacciando il nemico . . . .

Here in the bloody fields where the bayonet is in front, we attack pushing the enemy away. . . .

Fatevi avanti o vile o falsi se credete di aver un cuore singero

Come forward (I command) all of you who are cowardly or false (if you believe) if you have a sincere heart.

Mentre si occupava il Monte Nero voi dormivati sui letti Bianchi

While we occupied Black Mountain all of you slept in your white beds

e in conclusione rinegate con mente risculdata di sampagne chianti?

And in conclusion all of you reneged, was your mind warmed from champagne or chianti?

Author Commentary
1. Because we feel your pain, we have a clean conscience.

diceste il vero case da zitelloni e da molinorn non e' così che si conquista il monte nero, il san Michele il san Martino monfalcone il monte sei busi santa maria santa Lucia il vodil ed i forti di Tolmino. Sulla piazza urladate viva la guerra o brutti scellerati e pannulloni venite qui che e' vostra terra dove l'Austria ha piazzato dei cannoni avanti qui sono i vostri averi o scellerati? d'andare a Trieste e questo il momento su venite date avanti a prendere Gorizia. ma voi non siete dun cuore civile di dare esempio alla vostra idea. Su via impugnati un fucile e raggiungete un corpo alla trincea. Ma questo non lo fate o gente sporca perchè siete ingiusti della vita e degni del paese della forca e di strappardi le unghe dalle dita. Finitela una di volta o disgraziati

---

Author Commentary

1. Each of these small towns was the scene of a fierce battle. The Austrians had months to prepare defensive positions. They used to their advantage several ancient mountaintop forts. Their trenches, troops, and artillery held the high ground. The Austrians were outnumbered three to one, with their strategic advantages, and with the use of

Nei vostri comuni non dicate il vero case da zitelloni e da Molino . . .

In your towns you do not tell the truth as (gossiping, lying low class), old bachelors

Non è cose che si conquista il monte nero,il san Michele il san Martino monfalcone il monte sei busi santa maria santa lucia il dodil ed i forti di Folmino.[1]

This is not the way to conquer Black Mountain, San Michael, San Martino, Monfalcone, mount Sei Busi, Saint Mary, Saint Lucia, the dodil and the forts of Folmino.

Sulla piazza urlavate viva la Guerra

On the town square all of you shouted, "Long live the war."

o brutti sciellerati e fannulloni venite qui che è vostra terra dove

Oh you ugly, reprehensible, lazy ones, come here where it is your land

L'Austria fa riazzato dei cannoni avanti qui sono vostri avere o sciellerati?

The Austrians have placed a lot of cannons in front of your land, oh you reprehensible ones?

D'andare a Trieste è questo il momento su venite la tevi avanti a prendere Gorizia

To go to Trieste is this the time to go forward to take Gorizia?

Ma voi non siete dun cuore civile di dare esempio alla vostra idea[3]

But you are not a civil heart to give example to your ideas

Su via impegna ti un lucile e ranggiungeti un corpo all trimcea.

Come on grab a rifle and become a body in the trenches.

Ma questo non lo fate o gente sporca perchè sieti ingiasti della vita e dengni del parco della forca e di strapparvi le unghe dale dita.

But you will not do this you dirty people because you are unjust in life and you design the park for the gallows where fingernails are pulled from the fingers.

Fine te la uan volt o disgraziati

End it once and for all, you disgraced people.

artillery from fortified mountain positions, the Italians suffered greatly. The Italians did not have a shortage of manpower, however, they lacked almost every supply an attacking army requires. Food, ammunition, and artillery were scarce. Most acutely, they lacked competent leadership resulting in enormous and unnecessary loss of life. It is estimated that four Italians were killed for every yard of ground gained

2. I think he means to say that those with the good heart are at the front and the lazy, reprehensible ones who are cheering this war on are at home, not in range of cannons.

3. In other words all of you do not have the courage of your convictions. You are not willing to lead at the front, you are willing to lead from the rear.

guardate dove la morte ci sorprende che siamo macellati da corpi umani. Voi siete al sicuro o miserabili e non sentite i lamenti. Chi è colui che sia dichiarati in abili? Forse sieti tubercolosi ciechi zoppi oppure gobbi? Dovete fare la cara delle nostre fatiche ricuperandoci con simili ventri allora si che sarebbe un bel boccone per i Tedeschi. Se voi userete a prendere parte su Trento o Trieste, sarà una buona ricompensa per voi di questa guerra. La bella gioventù robusta e sana dovete perire per le vostre idee e voi tenendolo a vostra disposizione le miglior donne della gioventù novella. Sulla Tomba dei poveri soldati germoglieranno coltivati e rinvigorite col redente sole questi fiori si ricorderanno affinché di voi non sarà fatto vendetta.

Fine Godiny 14/12 1917

Guardate dove la morte ci sorprende che siamo macellati

Look where we are surprised with death where we are butchered

Ti da corpi umani,

The war gives you human bodies.

Voi siete al sicuro o miserabili e non sendite i lamenti[1]

You are safe you miserables, and you don't hear the laments

Chi è colui che dia dichiarati abili? Forse siete tubercolosi

Who declared you disabled? Perhaps you have tuberculosis?

ciechi zoppi loppure gobbi? Doveti fare la cura della nostre fati iche ricomerandosi[2]

Blind, lame or hunched back? You must give the cure to our fatigue so we can recuperate.

Con simili nostri all'ora si che sarebbe un bel boccone per i Tedeschi . . .

At that point that it would be like a sweet dessert for the Germans . . .

Se voi userete a prendere parte su Trento Trieste, sarà una buona ricompensa per noi di quest querra

If all of you would take part in the trenches of Trieste, it would be a good repayment for us in this war.

La bella gioventù robusta e sana dovete perire per le vostri idee

The beautiful young and healthy people must perish for your ideas.

E voi tenendo a vostra d'isposizione le migliore donne della gioventù novella[3]

And you are keeping at your disposal the best of the young people.

Sulla tomba dei poveri soldati germoglieranno coltivati e rinvigorite col redente sole questi fiore vi ricorderano

On the tomb (grave) of the poor soldiers will grow cultivated and reinvigorated with redemption by the sun flowers that will remind you of us

affinche di voi non sarà fatto vendetta.

It will not be a revenge.

Fine Goding 14/12/1917

The end Goding 14/12/1917

Author Commentary

1. the anguished cries of the dying
2. Come take our places in the trenches for a while so we can rest
3. Novella refers to the freshest, the newest, the best, often used in reference to new wine

Canzonetta funebre

Di quel marmo che inchiude lospoglio

Di quel figlio che più non vedrò

e nella Tomba raccolgo lospoglio

d'unna madre che tanto l'amò;

    T'alledai fra gli astenti e daffanni

    Toccò il destino lovuole così

e non avendo compiuto i dentanni

innocente inguerra morì...

Dovesei? perché non rispondi:

La tua madre languisce perte

    le tue labbra divine gioconde.

non potranno baciarmi mai più.

    Compatite una povera madre

cha aperso il figlio sul fior dell'età

e compiagete il vecchio suo padre

che anche; Tedeschi farebbero pietà.

    Zims Goding il 15/12 917

Cansonetta funebre
"Che Anche; Tedeschi Farebbero Pieta"

Little Funeral Song
"Even the Germans Would Have Pity"

Di quell marmo che rinchiude le spoglie

Di quell figlio che più non vedrò

E nella tomba raccolgo lospoglio

D'unna madre che tanto l'amò

T'allevai tra gli stenti e l'affani

Toccò il destino lo vuole cosi

e non avendo compiuto i ventanni

Innocente in Guerra mori,

Dove sei? Non rispondi

La tua madre languisec per tè

Le tue labra divine gioconde,

non potranno baciarmi mai più

Compatite una povera madre

Cha perso il figlio sul for dell'età

e compiangete il Vecchio suo padre

Che anche; Tedeschi farebbero pieta.

Fine Goding. Il 15/12/1917

Of that marble that encloses the remains.

Of that son that I will no longer see.

In the tomb I collect the remains

Of a mother that loved him so much.

I raised you between hardships and worry

He touched fate; he wants it like this.

He had not even turned twenty years old.

Innocent, in war he died.

Where are you? Why do you not answer?

Your mother is languishing for you

Your divine joyful lips.

they will not be able to kiss me again.

Pity a poor mother.

She has lost the son in the bloom of life.

and pity the old man, his father.

Even the Germans would have pity.

The end Goding. Il 15/12/1917

Ogni Madre che al suo figlio vuol bene
quello che soffre il suo cuore fosa
e sara morto che... orribile penna
il mio figlio sul fior dell'età

Se potessi scavar di una fossa
aseppellirmi vorrei dame'
per poter collocarle mie ossa
solo un palmo lontano da te.

Ola mattina il cancello si apre
ett'io son sempre laprima all'entrar.
la dove rimane la salma del morto
perpoter al mio figlio parlare

Alla sera il cancello sichiude
ett'il guardiano mimpone diuscir.
io son costretta ala sciar questa terra
ma il mio cuore però s'resta qui

Fine

Ogni madre che al suo figlio vuol bene	Every mother that really loves her son,
Quello che sofre il suo cuore fosa	Knows how her heart suffers
E sara morto che orrible penne	He would have died in horrible pain.
Il mio figlio sul fior dell'età[1]	My son in the bloom of his age.
Se potessi scavar di una fossa	If I could dig a grave
A seppelirmi vorrei da mè	I would like to bury myself
Per poter collocarle mie ossa	To be able to put my bones in it.
Solo un palino lontano da te.[2]	Just a palm away from you.
Alla mattina il canello si apre[3]	In the morning the gate opens.
Ett'io son semper la prima al'entrar	I am always the first to enter
La dove rimane la salma del morto	Where are the bodies of the dead remains.
Per poter al mio figlio parlar.	To be able to speak to my son.
Ett la sera il cancello si chinde	In the evening the gate closes.
Ett' il guardiano mimpone di usci	The guardian forces me to go out.
Io son costretta a la sciar questa terra[4]	I am forced to stay in this land,
Ma il mio cuore però resta qui.	But my heart remains here.[5]
Fine.	The end.

Author Commentary

1. Early youth
2. Within a short reach
3. cemetery gate
4. "This land" refers to the homeland of the dead soldier.
5. I think he means that the mother's heart remains with her son, even though his remains are far away in a tomb/grave in Austria. These passages are a bit difficult to follow in that Fedele change perspective from a third person narrative to that of the dead soldier, to the view of the grieving mother and father. It seems to me that he is not describing just one death. I think he sees this grief as recurring tens of thousands of times in Italy, Austria, and all of Europe. Despite much being lost in translation, Fedele's depth of compassion for a grieving mother is evident. How could he not visualize his own mother and father living through this kind of grief?

Figure 34: Postcard of funeral in snow

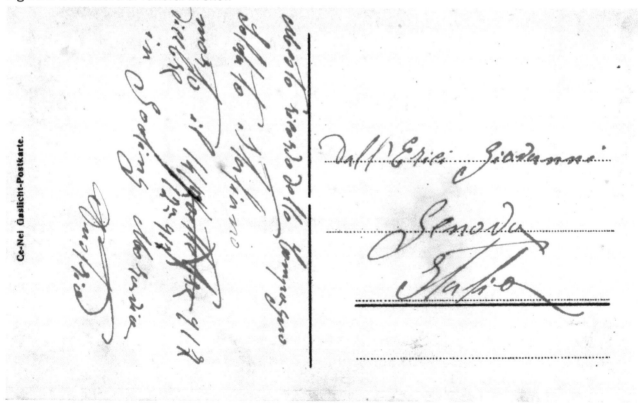

Figure 35: Reverse of postcard of funeral in snow

The photos on these two postcards of funerals appear to have been taken at the same location. The similarities include the building with the same windows, the upright cross near the coffin, and large white ribbons. The inscription on the reverse of the first postcard translates *Giovanni Erici Our*

Figure 36: Postcard of funeral on brown grass

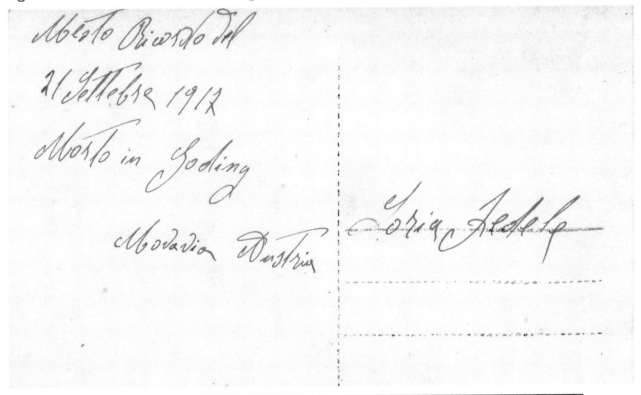

Figure 37: Reverse of postcard of funeral on brown grass, signed by Fedele Loria.

memory of friend and Italian soldier, dead 14 December 1917 in Goding. The inscription on the reverse of the second postcard translates *Our memory of 21 September 1917 dead in Goding Movavia Austria.* This postcard was signed by *Fedele Loria.*

Postcard of prisoner Lutera at Goding 28 May 1917.

"Memory of our imprisonment in Goding 28 May, 1917, Greetings and Kisses."

Figure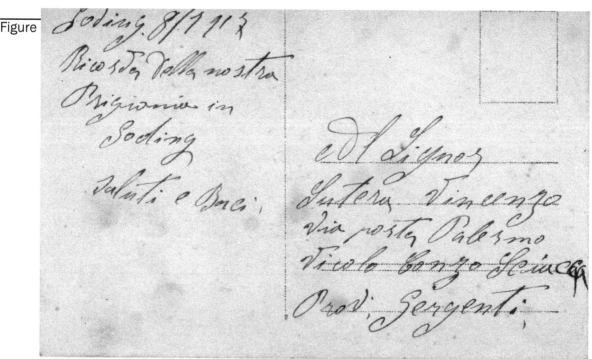

Figure 39: Reverse of postcard of prisoner Lutera

Postcard of prisoner Martiorana at Goding 28 May 1917.

"Memory of our imprisonment in Goding

28 May 1917 Greetings and kisses."

Figure 40: Postcard of prisoner Martiorana

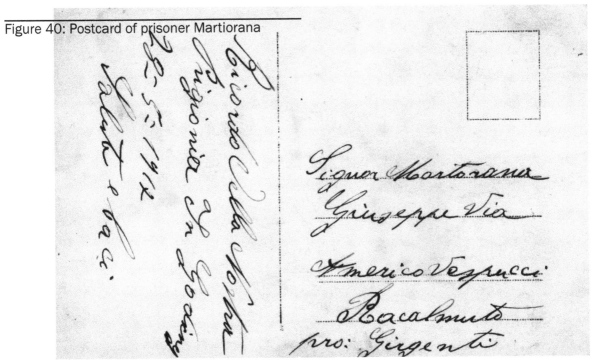

Figure 41: Reverse of postcard of prisoner Martiorana

(dispiacere d'una sposa) Godino il 16/11/29_

Mi rammento quel giorno che t'iannunsia d'avan che eri
richiamato   dodendo far quella triste partenza
~~col settantesimo deviste~~ Lasciando la Moglie e una bambina
col settantesimo deviste assegnato che a Firenze aveva la residenza.

Triste è il destino la sorte ti toccò dovendo partire
lontano da me, fier Mazzoglioso di giovin Militar
partisti per la guerra. anche per guerreggiar.

Mirammento quella notte fatale che è avesso quel gran
combattimento, e tu riportasti una ferita mortale che
dovette spirar fra gran turmento. Chi di quante e molte
dolte chiamastenee dovendo spirar in quel crudel dolor

Triste è il destino prendesti il marito amee per non più
riportasmelo miscoppia il cuore ame.

Quando alla notte misogno mipar sempre la tua visione
quando misveglio oche Dana in lusione pensando al Marito mio
lassu lontano mori.. Quando la bimba tua Chiama
suo mamma stringendola e baciandola le dice
.

Dispiacere di unna Sposa

"O Mamma dove io mio Pappà?"

Goding il 16/12/1917

Mi ramminto quel giorno che ti aunisia

Che eri richimato. Dovendo far quella triste partenza

Lasciando la moglie e una bambina

Al settantesiomo vemiste assegnato che a Firenze aveva la residenza

Triste e il destino la sorte ti toccò dovendo partire

Lontano da me. Fier margoglioso di giovin military partiti per la guerra anche per guerreggiar

Mirammento quella note fatale che è sucesso

quell gran combattemente, e tu riportasti una ferita mortale che dovette spirar fra gran turmento.

Chi si quante e molte volte chiamati me dovendo spirar in quell crudel dolor

Triste e il destino prendesti il maritto amce per non più riportamelo

mi sccoppia il cuore a me.

Quando alla note misogno mipar sempre la tua visione

quando mi sveglio oche dana inlusione pensando al marito mio

lassu lontano mori . . .

quando la bimmba ti chiama sua mamma

Stringendola e baciandola le dice

O mamma dove il mio pappà

The Sorrow of a Bride

"Oh Mother, where is my father?"

Goding 16/12/1917

I remember that day they announced that[7]

Were recalled[2] Having to make that sad departure.

Leaving the wife and baby girl.

You were assigned to the seventieth divi—sion because you lived in Florence where they[3] had residence.

Sad is the destiny, the fate that you were having to leave

Far from me. You were a proud young military man. You left for the war and for combat.[4]

I remember that fatal night that it happened

that big battle, and you bore a mortal wound that made you die in great torment.

Who knows how much and often you called out to me that you were dying in that cruel pain?

Sad is the destiny that takes your hus—band, my friend, they were not able to bring him back to you.

It bursts/breaks my heart.

When during the night I dream, your face always appears to me.

when I awake also from the illusion thinking of my husband

who died so far away . . .

When the little girl asks her mother

Hold her and kiss her when she says

Oh mother, where is my father

lassu nel paradisoper la patria dovete lui partire

Sul campo della gloria il padre tuo mori,

Chissa quanti morti lassu resto

Lasciando le famiglie nel crudel dolor.

Chi perde il padre e chi il figlio il marito

ancor non avremmo mai provato cose dolor al cuore

Fine

Up there in Heaven. For his country he had to leave.

Your father died on the field of glory.

Who knows how many died and stayed up there?

Leaving the families in cruel pain.

Who knows who lost his father, and who a son, the husband

They never had such a deep pain in their hearts.

The end

Author Commentary

1. you had to go
2. to military service
3. the 70th regiment
4. wife's perspective

AUTHOR NOTE

The Tongue of Women

Six years after the war, Fedele met his wife in WV and was happily married to her for nearly fifty years. His daughters told me he had the utmost respect for his wife and unlimited love for his five girls. We know from his writing that he had an immense love for his mother and sisters. When you read Fedele's next chapter, you might get the impression that he would not be a loving husband and respectful father. If we view this chapter through the lens of male superiority that existed 100 years ago, his stereotyped opinions would have found a receptive audience among some men. Even by the standards of those days, he would have offended many men and every woman. In today's age of equal rights for women, he certainly would have been run out of town for expressing such beliefs. I believe he was indulging in a lot of exaggerated stereotypes.

Per te, per te nato a vivere
in un'Italia più forte, più felice, più rispettata

Postcard of prisoner Pecchia at Goding 15 July 1917.

Reverse of Postcard of prisoner Pecchia at Goding 15 July 1917. Goding memories of our imprisonment Greetings.

Figure 42: Postcard of prisoner Pecchia

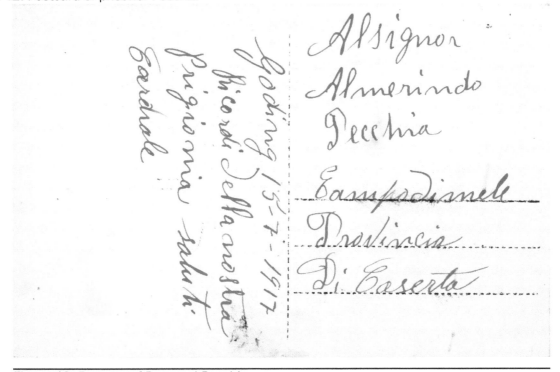

Figure 43: Reverse of Postcard Pecchia

O mamma dove il mio Pappà   lassù nel   paradiso
che per la patria dovette lui partire sul campo della gloria
Il padre tuo morì   Chissa quanti morti lassù resto
lasciando le famiglie nel crudel dolor.

Chi perde il Padre e chi il figlio il Marito
ancor non avranno mai provato così dolor al cuore

Fine

La lingua delle donne.

E la lingua delle donne e la cagione d'ogni male e la
rovina universale d'ogni popolo e massima. Incostante
e men vognire capriciose et vidiosi vanitose e
turgogliose la natura vi creò. Pater noster) et
in casa sempre intante acchiacchierare e basimare
vi te mostre dell'Iferno, Peggio ancora.)
Se qualcun viconfidasse un secreto delicato dopo
ancora gia svelato doi ludeti spopolato.
in Terra e in ciel) Et la mattina appena
giorno i capeli intricciati con cerotto con

La Lingua Delle Donne
"Statte Attenti Giovanetti"

E la lingua delle donne e la cagione di ogni male e la rovina universale dogni popolo e massiona,

incostante e men sognire capriciose et vidiosi vanitose e turgogliose la natura vi creò,

Pater noster!

et in casa sempre intante acchiacchierare e basimare

Siete moster dell'inferno. Peggio ancora,

Se qualcun vi confidosse un secreto delicato

Dopo un ora giu svelato voi laveti spopolato in terra e in ciel,

Nella mattina aprena giorno

i capelli intricciati con cerotto e con

The Tongue of Women
"Be Careful Young Men"

The tongue of women is the reason of everything evil and the universal ruin of every population and mission and proud, nature created you.

Inconsistent women capricious liars and envious and vain

Our Father!

And at home always talking too much and blaming.

You are monsters of hell. Worse yet.

If someone confides in any of you a deli—cate secret

After an hour all of you have revealed it to all the people on earth and in heaven.

In the morning as the day begins

your hair is braided with metal hair clips and with

Author Commentary

1. In exasperation, an Italian might say, "momma mia." Here, he very sarcastically uses the latin expression for "Our Father" instead of momma mia, in what I think may be a very brief pleading prayer to our heavenly father.

pomata e ferretti inguantita) un bel petto
rimolato rimolato il rosso naturale e le mode ingene
rale voi sapete è solo amar.) Ha mia moglie una
gran donna impolitica dottrina ma una lingua sopertina
più tagliente dell'acciaio)) ma col mio rubito
Baston che si sente e mai non parta io cerco di
dimarla ma invece, mi mori)) Statte attenti
giovanotti quando moglie prendere vi pentirete, non
vorrete dopo fatto il gran error.
Statte attenti giovanotti se la moglie e chiacchierona
Bugiarda chiacchierona che vi cerco di ingannare,
son venato espressamente, che profitto di tutto
questo è un bel sermone che profitto di dara
vi voi donne tutte quante vecchie e ditte
maritate se vi offesa perdonate che il poeta
vi lo do?

Fine Goding. il 18/12/1917

pomata e ferretti inquantità. Un bel letto	ointment and a lot of underwires/hair pins. A nice bed.
Simolato il rossre naturale e le mode ingene	You simulate naturally red hair and the ingenious fashions.
Ma le voi sapete solo amari,¹	But you know only bitter.
Fa mia moglie una gran donna impolitica dotrine ma una lingua serpertina più tagliente dell'acciais.	Make me a wife, a grand woman with—out political doctrine, but with a serpent's tongue that is sharper than steel.
Ma col mio subito tone che si sente e mai non parla io cerca	But with my tone (of voice) she immedi—ately feels (knows) she should not speak, is (the woman) is seek.
Statte Attenti giovanettti quando moglie prendere te se pentirvi,	Be careful young men when you take a wife if you don't want to repent,
non vorerete dopo fatto il gran errori.	You won't want it after you make the big mistake is already made.
State attenti giovanotti se la moglie e chiacchierona	Be careful young men if your wife is a chatterbox
se Bugiarda chiacchierona che vi cerca di ingunare	if she is a lying chatterbox that tries to cheat
Son Venuto espressamente per cantar la canson	I came here expressly to sing the song
Questo e un vero bel sermon che profitto vi sarà	This is a really nice sermon. What a profit it will be
A voi donne tutte quante vecchie e ditte maritato	to all you old ladies who say you are married?
se Dio fleso perdonate che il poeta	(Please) God come down and forgive (me) the poet
di lo Do?	who is telling (the truth)
Fine Goding il 18/12/1917	The end, Goding, 18/121917

Author Commentary

1. Perhaps he meant bitterness, which in Italian is amarezza.

Figure 44: Group photo at unknown occasion

The back of this photo is blank, so the occasion for this gathering is unknown. We can't read the sign because the men on the ground are blocking the view. There are several young women in this photo, so it was probably made while Fedele was stationed in Milan after the war. Fedele is in the second row, just left of center.

AUTHOR'S NOTE

Come Closer, Come Closer, to Me

The Christmas season of 1917 touched him deeply. We see this in a flurry of five entries dated December 24. His emotions range widely from idyllic happiness to shock, and then hopefulness in "Spinci Spinci ame." In "Little Song of the Women," he temporarily escapes a harsh reality with some fantasy about women. There is self-pity and fervent prayer in "Orphan Without a Roof." He displays deep feelings of compassion for his mother in "From the Memory of a Prisoner." There is sarcastic cheerfulness while others are quietly sobbing in "Oh Body of all the Devils." This wide range of mixed emotions

Figure 45: Close-up of group photo, Fedele in 2nd row left of center.

spilled out of his heart, through his hand, and onto paper. Collectively, these entries allow us to see the essence of Fedele. They are the window to his heart on one of the darkest days of his life.

Fedele's next poem, "Spinci Spinci ame" (Come closer, come closer, to me), is entirely different from everything else in his diary. He uses a different sentence structure, rhythm, meter, and subject matter. Because this poem is so different, Daniela Frugis did some research to determine if this poem was written by someone else. We wondered if perhaps he copied it or paraphrased it from memory. He did not plagiarize it. It is possible that parts of the poem have their origins in childhood memories. I believe he found the inspiration to write this poem from another poet. Umberto Saba was a well-known Italian poet in the first half of the twentieth century with more than 600 published poems. Many of them were about soldiers and their experiences during the first world war. I feel certain that Fedele read some of those poems. A couple of Fedele's chapter titles reflect some of the same themes used in Saba's poetry. One of Saba's poems, in particular, stands out. He wrote of a weary soldier on leave from the front lines. The day is gray, the clouds low, far from the roar of the cannons, and boredom rules him. He is without joy or terror. The soldier sits in a little house, at a desk with a blank piece of paper. He is devoid of inspiration about what to write. He prays to God to inspire his hand to explain the mystery of life. But the inspiration does not come. Every writer has sat in front of a blank piece of paper, waiting for inspiration. Saba owes success as a poet in part to his experiences during the war. Saba wrote from the heart. Thousands of soldiers and their families could directly relate to his words. At the time this was written, Fedele, like Saba, was a weary soldier, far from the roar of the cannons and certainly without joy or terror. On a winter day in the alps, the clouds would often be low and gray. Life as a prisoner would, at times, be very boring. We know Fedele was a soldier, a writer, and a poet. How could he not relate to the circumstances described by Saba? He would completely understand Saba's struggle with inspiration on a dreary, boring day in captivity, far from joy or terror. Saba ends his poem in the following manner:

Passeggiamo in un giardino—*We are strolling in a park/garden*

Un grazioso soldatino—*A kind, gracious young soldier*

In the last two lines, Saba is offering an idea, an inspiration to the reader. He wants the reader to pick up the idea and craft a story about a young soldier in the garden. Fedele positions himself in the poem as the soldier. It is a tragic story that, in the end, holds hope for a better future.

This poem can be interpreted in a few different ways. Some have said that Fedele simply used his imagination to continue the story as inspired by Saba. Others remembered songs that their grandmother would sing to the little children. Fedele would have heard and remembered such childhood songs and rhymes. They say he is blending those childhood memories with his imagination to create this beautiful poem. I think Fedele took the idea and expanded it with his experiences and memories. He dreams that he is in a courtyard/garden. There is a young woman/nanny who is singing a nursery rhyme to a little boy. This is an idyllic setting, an innocent and pleasant set of circumstances. The young soldier is observing this happy scene and is drawn closer to her and the child. Suddenly this idyllic scene in the garden is interrupted by a superior officer/military duty that disrupts his life. He is shocked to learn that he has been arrested and confined. At the end of his poem, he holds the hope to one day return to her and to a happy life.

The result is a poem that blossomed into a fitting metaphor for this period of his life.

Spinci

Passeggiando in un giardino
Un grazioso soldatino
si vedette in un sedile
si mostrada assai gentile
E dunna Bambinaia
che aveda l'aia molto gaia
con un picin
giocando ognor.
Cantada una canzona
che forma l'attenzione
del soldatin.
Fermò a sentir
Mio bel picin
spinci spinci spinci a me
Tira tira tira ute
uno due e tre.
Pian piannino il soldatino

Spinci Spinci ame

Passeggiamo in un giardino[1]

Un grazioso soldatino

Si sedette in un sedile

Si mostrava assai gentile

Ed una Bambinaia[2]

Che aveva l'aia molto goia.[3]

Con un picin[4]

Giocando ognor[5]

Cantava una canzona[6]

Che forma la attenzione

Del soldatino

Fermò a sentir[7]

Mio bel picin

Spinci spinci spinci ame

Tira tira tira ate

Uno due e tre

Pian piammino il soldatino

Come closer to me, Come closer to me, to me

We are strolling in a garden

A gracious young soldier

He is observing the scene while seated.

His appearance was kind and gentle

And a nanny

She was very happy

With a little one

They are playing a game

She was singing a song.

That holds the attention

Of the young soldier

I stop to listen

My dear little one

Come closer to me, come closer
to me, to me

Pull me closer to you, pull me closer to
you, to you.

One two and Three

Slowly, slowly the young soldier

Author Commentary

1. A botanical garden or a carefully tended courtyard.
2. She is caring for a little boy. I suspect he would picture her as young and attractive.
3. For her, it was joyous to be there. She was playing with the little boy.
4. picin is a term of endearment for a small child.

Continued on pg 95

minci   a me

si accostava più vicino.

Abla Bella Bambinaia

Che dell'aria molto gaia

Di cca frottole o migliaia

che mentre essa cantava

Un tenente li passava

E il   soldatin

Fra il si e il no

Non si pottete alzar

Per porterlo salutare

Perchè il pilin

Dica così

Mio soldatin

spinci spinci spinci a me

tira tira tira a te

Uno due e tre

E il forbo tenentino

Si accostava più vicino	approaches closer
Della bella bambinaia[8]	To the beautiful nanny.
Che dell'aria molto gaia[9]	With of feeling of much joy
Di ceva frottole o migliaia	????????
Che mentre essa cantava	Then while she sang
Un tenente li passava	A lieutenant passed by there
E il soldatino	And the young soldier
Fra il si e il no	Between yes and no
Non si pottete alzar[10]	You can't get up
Per porterlo salutare	To make a salute?
Perchè il picin	Because of the little boy
Dicca così[11]	She went on like this,
Mio soldatin	My young soldier
Spinci spinci spinci ame	Come closer, come closer come closer to me
Tira tira tira a te	Pull me, pull me, pull me to you.
Uno due e tre	One two and Three
E il forbo tenentino	And the sneaky young lieutenant

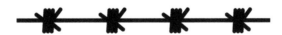

5. Playing with each other.

continued from page 93

6. She was singing a children's song to the little boy.
7. As she sings to the boy
8. Young lady
9. He was very pleased to be there and see this
10. He may be using some poetic license here. He does not give a reason as to why he did not stand up to salute the lieutenant.
11. the nanny continued singing

si accostava al soldatino
Egli disse sei in aresto
In caserma vai presto
E non fai ne anche un gestino
E il povero soldato
si sentì mortificato
Perchè il picin
più non scherzò!
E disse alla Bambinaia
già d'all'aria non più gaia
La vengo aimè
tranquillo ch di stà
Ma certo io sono
Che gli tornerò a giocar
se come alla prigione
lo fate entrar.

Udine Godiny 24/12 1917

Si accostava al soldatino	He said you are under arrest.
Egli dice sei in aresto	He approached the toy soldier
In caserma vai presto	Go to the barracks immediately.
E non fai neanche un gestino[1]	And don't make even a little gesture.
E il povero soldato	And the poor soldier
Si senti mortifaicato[2]	He felt mortified.
Perchè il picin	Because of the little boy
Pi`u non scherzo!	I am not joking!
E disse all baminaia	And he said to the nanny
Gia d'all'aria non piu goia	The air of joy was gone
La vengo ai me	(Oh no)I go there (to the barracks)
Tranqullo si stà	Stay calm,
Ma certo io sono	But I am certain, I know
Che gli tornerò a giocar	(The child says) I will return to play
Se come alla prigione	Even if you are in a prison
Lo fate entrar.[3]	I will enter
Fine Goding 24/12/1917	The End Goding 24/12/1917

Author Commentary

1. Do not be insubordinate, you are guilty
2. He wanted to die
3. Don't be sad
4. I will go to the prison to play with you there.

Postcard of prisoner Basilio at Goding at Goding 29 May 1917.

"Memory of imprisonment in Goding

Greeting and Kisses."

Figure 47: Reverse of postcard of prisoner Basilio

AUTHOR'S NOTE

In "Little Song of the Women," Fedele describes in detail his impressions of various women from around the globe. I have made a careful study of this chapter. After consulting with Daniella, Father Anthony, Aldo, and others, we have concluded that Fedele is really putting his imagination to work as he describes the characteristics and attributes of the women he has met in his "ten years and six months of travels around the world." Here in this chapter, Fedele as a writer utilizes his poetic license to its full potential. Some of the ways he describes women from various countries seem to be exaggerated or stereotypical. It is possible he may have seen magazines or newspapers that may have inspired his ideas about these foreign and exotic women. He writes, "British women are pale, quiet, and cold-natured. Spanish women are feisty and jealous. African women are scary." Fedele likely traveled all over Italy while in the Army. He would have had personal experiences, as he describes the women of Napoli, Florence, Torino, Sicily, Calabria, Milan, and other parts of Italy. I don't know if he was a "ladies' man," but in some ways, it seems that he writes from experience.

I believe he may have met a few women from different countries in his travels. He was fifteen years old when he came to America for the first time. During those early years, he was raised in a strict Catholic home. Because San Giovanni is a remote mountain town in Calabria, it is unlikely that he had any exposure to women from exotic locations such as Arabia or Japan. During the next two and a half years of his life, he was a coal miner in the hills of West Virginia. He certainly would have met some African American women there. The next four years, he was in the army. During much of his enlisted time, he would have been living in the trenches. His diary was written during his twenty-first year while in captivity. It seems that he had a lot of idle time as a POW. I would not be surprised if a young man with time on his hands would let his mind wander to thoughts of exotic women and their various attributes. This type of creative writing probably would be a pleasant distraction from his circumstances. Perhaps writing this chapter brought him some much-needed mental relief from the stresses of captivity, the threat of beatings, and the harsh reality of starvation.

Canzonetta

1ª Il mondo ho girato
Dieci anni e sei mesi
Per mille paesi
ferma mi son
Per quanto ho veduto
Di grande varietà
Le donne ho ammirato
Con grande attenzione
Dei loro costumi
Vi voglio parlare
E state ascoltare
Le varie impresioni

2ª Le donne spagnole
Dagli occhi luccenti
Coi fianchi sporgenti
E sono così
Modensi e superbe

Canzonetta delle Donne
"Son Fiore Gentile"

Little Song of the Women
"They are Gentle Flowers"

1a Il mondo lo girato

Dieci anni e sei mesi

Per mille paesi

Ferma mi

Per quanto lo veduto

Le donne ho ammirato

Con grand attenzione

Dei loro costume

Vi volgio parlare[1]

E stati ascoltare[2]

Le vari impersioni

2a Le donne spagnole

Dagli occhi luccenti

Cui fin chi sporgenti

E son cosi

Movensi e superbe[3]

1a I have been around the world

For ten years and six months

In many countries

I stopped.

For a great variety of things, I have seen

I have admired women

With a lot of close attention.

To their ways (mannerisms)

I want to say to you

And you will listen.

To the different various impressions.

2a The Spanish women

With their eyes sparkling

You can see their curvaceous hips.

And they are like this

They are alive, moving and proud.

Author Commentary

1. voglio is the same as: "I very strongly want"
2. This is less of a request and more of a command.
3. Probably he is referring to flamenco dancers.

Continued on pg 103

delle donne
Delle donne
Nature focose
amanti gelose
Che sonno ammazzar
Se amor chiedete
Vi guardano avanti
Senz'oro e brillanti
Non vaporano il cor.
3° Le donne Francese
Per chi le conosce
son come briose
Nel latte e Caffè
Odorano in bocca
Di dentro e di fuori
Per ricchi signori
Son dolci bocconi
Serviti in merenda

Delle donne	Of the women
Nautue focose	They have a very feisty nature.
Amanti gelose	They are very jealous.
Che sonno ammazzar[4]	In a loving way they are jealous.
Le amor chedete	If you ask them about love
Vi guardano avanti	They will look past you
Senz' oro e brillanti	Without gold and precious stones
Non daprono il cor[5]	They will not give their heart.
3a Le donne Francese	3a The French women
Per chi le conoscie	If you know them
Son come briose[6]	They are like brioche
Nel latte e Caffè	Just like milk in coffee.
Odorano in bocca	Like the aroma in your mouth
Di dentro e di fuori	Both inside and outside
Per ricchi signori	For rich men
Son dolci Bocconi[7]	They are like the sweet treats.
Serviti a merenda[8]	Served as an afternoon snack.

continued from page 101

4. They will fight the other woman if she is jealous.
5. As Elizabeth Taylor said, "Diamonds are a girl's best friend." Taken all together, Fedele takes a decidedly negative tone in his view of the Spanish women.
6. A French pastry that you dip in milk or coffee
7. They are beautiful little morsels
8. Merenda does not translate to English. You could say it is a snack for leisurely rich men at around 5:00 pm.

Comprandole in piazza
Del latte la tazza
Vi fanno leccar.
4ª Le bionde inglesine
stecchite fierre
glaciate notturne
Nel far l'amor.
Ma il sangue non bolle
A far colle molle
Lo sanno pigliar.
Una foglia d'abione
Di tutto se secca
La sola Bistecca
La secca un pochin.
5ª Per quanto sappiamo
le donne olandesi
son molte cortese
Nel far l'amore.

Comprando le in piazza	You can buy them in the square
Del latte la tazza	Like milk in a cup
Vi fanno lecar[1]	They make you lick the cup.
4a Le bionde inghessine[2]	4a The blonde English ladies
Stecchite ficure[3]	They look like stick figures
glaciate nature	they are glacial
Nel fur lamore	In the way they make love.
Ma il sangue non bolle[4]	But the blood is not boiling.
A far colle molte	They do not have a lot of enthu—siasm in bed
Lo sanno pigiliari	They take sex with no enthusiasm
Una foglia a	A dried leaf
Di tutto se secca	Everything is dry
La sola Bistecca	A steak
La sceea un pochin[5]	The steak is dry.
5a Per quanto sappiamo	5a For what we know about
Le donne olendesi	The women of Holland
Son molte cortese	They are very gentle
Nel far l'amore	And ready to make love.

Author Commentary

1. They are like the sweet little bit of drink on the side of the cup. You are tempted to lick the side of the cup. Fedele is very positive in his outlook on the French women. They are sweet bites. Unfortunately, only the rich men have the sweet ones.
2. The cute chicks
3. Are slender (skinny)
4. They don't get hyper or excited. They are not hot-blooded like the Spanish or Italian women.

Continued on pg 107

Si mettano molto
Di pesce salato
Di stocco affamato
E di   Baccalà
Di sale elemento
non fanno lattenza
E qui la conseguenza
Ne stiamo a subir.
Per chi non conosce.
6ª Le donne Tedesche
Di pelle son fresche
son fresche di cuor.
I loro mariti
son gente d'affari
Perciò fanno affari
affari anche là
Così nell'amore
Signore ed artisti

Li mitrano molto	They eat a lot
Di pesce salato[6]	Of salted fish
Di stucco affamato	Of dried smoked cod
E di baccala[7]	And of baccala
Di sale elamento	Of the element salt
Non fanno la llenza	There is no shortage
E qui la consequenza	And here are the consequences
Ne stiamo o subir[8]	We will suffer
Per chi non coanosce[9]	For whoever does not know
6a Le donne Tedesche	6a The German women
Di pelle son fresch	They have soft fresh skin
Son fresche di cuor	They have soft fresh hearts
I loro mariti	Their husbands
Son gente d`affair	Are people of business.
Per ci`o fanno affair[10]	Therefore, they are doing business.
Affari anche la'	The way they make love is like the way they do business.
Cosi nell`amore[11]	Likewise they are the same in love.
Signore ed artisti	Ladies and artists

continued from page 105

5. An overcooked steak could have been good, but now it is dry.

6. baccala

7. dried fish

8. Suffer from eating too much salt

9. Some who eat too much salt do not know it is bad for you.

10. They care about business and money

11. The men do not care about love, and imprison women are not happy because the men are after money and not them.

Son tutte affarite
Di grande valor.
7ª Le donne lungheresе
Bellezze e profumi
Degli occhi sagaci
Di buono splendor
In loro dimora
E un uomo di gomma
Vorrebero dar,
E anno una lingua
Che ride e ferisce
Giamai non risista
alla pace non do...
8ª Le donne Africane
Le indigine vere
Di pelle son nere
fan brutte impresion
Le gambe scoperte

Son tutte affarite	They are all business
Di grande valor.[1]	Of great value
7a Le donne lungherese	7a The women from Hungary
Belelzze e profumi	Are beautiful and smell nice.
Degli occhi saguci	They have shrewd eyes
Di buono splendor	Of beautiful splendor
In loro dimura[2]	They are demur
E un uomo di gomma[3]	A man like a plaything
Verrebbero dari	Is what they want.
E anno una lingua	They have a tongue
Che ride e ferisce	Their tongue can laugh or wound you.
Siamai non risista[4]	Let it never be
Alla pace non ha	Or I will never have peace.
8a Le donne Africane	8a The African women
Le indigine vere	The real indigenous.
Di pelle son nere	With black skin
Fan brute impression	They make an ugly impression
Le gambe scoperte	Their legs are uncovered

Author Commentary

1. The women are of great value. Because they are businesswomen, they are very serious about business and making love.
2. shy
3. entertainment
4. God forbid
5. They don't wear bras, their breasts show freely

Continued on pg 111

Il naso schiacciato
Il labbro gonfiato
Il liber sen
Amar quelle donne
E un questo da pezzo
Al sol contatto
Mi fanno impresioni
9ª Le donne a Torino
son fiori gentili
Che le brezze d'aprile
che fanno in Brianz.
Di modu cortesi
Vacalgano bene
Se a mondo d'arene
Le state a mitar
Sarpenti lore fare
Con garbe le cose
Non sole le porte

Il naso schiacciato	The noses flattened
Il labro gonfiato	The lips are inflated.
Il liber sen[5]	The breasts are free
Amor quelle donne	To love these women
E un questo da pazzo[6]	This is craziness.
Al sol contatto[7]	The one contact.
Mi fanno impresioni[8]	They give me impressions.
9a Le donne a Torino	9a The women of Torino
Son fiore gentile	They are gentle flowers
Che le brezze d'Aprile	Like the breeze of April
Che fanno in briar	They make you feel like you are drunk
A moda cortesi	They have gentle ways
Vacalgano bene	They are worth something. They are of great value.
Le a mondo d'arene	The world of arenas
Le sta te a mitar	????????
Larpen ti lore fare	???????????????????
Con garbe le case	??????????the houses
Non sole le porte[9]	Not only the doors

6. Who ever loves these women are crazy.

continued from page 109

7. I have had only one contact with them.

8. The tone of this statement is that "They scare me." Or "They impress me in a negative way" a bad impression. I can't look at them, they disgust me.

9. A good guess at the tone of this passage is: If you do things in the way they like, then they will open their homes, their doors, and their hearts to you

Di aprono il cor.

10ª Le donne orientali
dal viso coperto
Nascondono certo
Di sotto un tesor
Chi usa scoprille
Oltragia il sultano
La legge il corano
Ma ometta il pascia
Solma baciai
e il turco del ghero
Il palo di ferro
Mi fece assagiar.

11ª Le donne giapponesi
In massa son brutte
Ma fumano tutte
E Bevono il tè.
Non mangiano carne

Di aprono il cor	They open the heart
10a Le donne orientali[1]	10a The oriental women
Dal viso coperot	Their face is covered
Anacondono certo	Hidden I am certain
Di sotto un tesor	Underneath is a treasure
Chi sua scoprille	If you dare to uncover them
Ol tragia il sultano	You will enrage the sultan
La legge il coran[2]	The law of the Muslims
Ma ometta il pascia[3]	But Mohammed the pascia
Io l una buciai	I kissed one
E il turio del ghero	And the (bodyguard)
Il palo di fero	The metal pole
Mi fece assagiar[4]	Made me test
11a Le donne giapponesi	11a The Japanese women
In mass son brute	Generally, they are ugly
Ma fumano tutte	But they all smoke
E beveno il te	And drink tea
Non mangiano carne	They don't eat meat

Author Commentary

1. Muslim women of the middle east, perhaps Arabia
2. It is the law
3. The pascia rules his own harem. He can remove the veil without breaking the law.
4. This passage is very difficult, a good guess would be he kissed one of the girls and the "ghero" bodyguard hit him with a steel rod.

Continued on pg 115

Son gialle di viso
Di pesce e di riso
Si nutrano ognor.
Badate che il pesce
Lo mangiano vivo
Ed è mi trido
Se frizzico un po'
12ª Le Belle Donnine
he stano a Milano
Ladorano a mano
Ed a macchina ancor.
Sartine e modiste
Bustaie e servette
Artiste e cocotte
Ne ho visto un milion
Faccine eleganti
Distinte in amore
Son larghe di amore

Son gialle di viso	They are yellow in their face
Di pesce e di rise	They eat fish and rice
Le mutrono ognor	They eat at any hour
Badate che il pesce[5]	Notice that the fish is alive.
Le mangiano vivo	They eat it alive
Ed è mi trivo	??????????????
Le frizzico un pò	It surprises—shocks me a little
12a Le belle donnine	12a The cute little women
Che stano a Milano	They are in Milan
Lavorano a mano	They work by hand
Ed a macchina ancora	And also with a sewing machine
Sartine e modiste[6]	they are tailors and fashion designers.
bustaie e servette	Uplifting bras and ?????
Artiste e cocotte[7]	Artists and cabaret dancers.
Ne ho visto un milan	I saw in Milan
Faccine elegante	Elegant faces
Distinte in amore	Distinct in love
Son large di amore	They are large in love

5. He may be referring to eating sashimi continued from page 113
6. Milan has always been the center of fashion and clothing design in Italy
7. Fedele may have been "a man about town" in Milan

E larghe di sen

13ª Le donne a Venezia

Nel loro dialetto

Vi fanno un effetto

Gradito a sentir

Di facile conquista

L'ò molto splendore

In gondola andrete

Con loro a remar

Al chiar di lunna

Vi fanno sostare

Ei larghi canali

Vi fanno passare.

14ª Quelle di Firenze

Dal debol seno

Qua non e lo stesso

che in altre città

Amore in pittura

E large di sen	And large in breasts
13a Le donne a Venezia	13a The women of Venice
Nel lor dialetto	With their dialect
Vi fanno un effettto	They make an impression
Gradito a sentire	Pleasant to listen to
Di facile Conquista	Very easy to conquer
L'o molto splendore	They are in their splendor
In goldola andrete	You will go with them in the gondola
Con loro a remar	Rowing with them
Al chiao di lunna	By the light of the moon
Vi fanno sostar	They make you stop
Ei larghi canali	The large canals
Vi fanno passare	They make you go through.
14a Quelle di Firenze	14a The ones in Florence
Dal deblo seno1	They have weak breasts.
Qua non e lo stesso	Here they are not the same
Che in alter città	Like in other cities.
Amore in pittura2	Love in painting

Author Commentary

1. small
2. they love art and painting

Continued on pg 119

di forme attraenti
di lingua eccellenti
Ne dano insegnari,
Passiamo alla donna
Che qui si distingue.
Almen con la lingua
Che sanno adoperar...
15ª Le donne di Roma
Per cui mi conoscono
Son tutte in profumo
Di dentro e di fuori
In dembi d'estate
Col troppo calore
Non Bolle l'amore
Con donne codi
Ma di questi sempre
Con questa stimezza
Qui la permanenzza
potrebbe durar.

Di farme attrenti[3]	Of beautiful form
Di lingua exccelenti[4]	They speak the language beautifully.
Ne sono insegnar[5]	They know how to teach.
Passiamo alla donna	Let's go to the woman
Che qui si distingque	That is so distinquished
che sanno adoperar[6]	At least with the language
Al men con la lingua	That they know how to use the tongue
15a Le donne di Roma	15a The women of Rome
Per cui mi conoscono	So they know me
Son tutte in profume.	They all use perfume.
In dempi l'estate	In the summer time
Col troppo calore	When it is really hot
Non Bolle l'amore[7]	love does not boil in them
Con donne cosi	With women like this
Ma di questi sempre[8]	but of these always
Con questa stimezza[9]	with this reason
Qui la permanenzza[10]	Here is permanence
Potrebbe durar.	It could last.

continued from page 117

3. They have nice figures, they are very attractive.
4. The modern Italian language has its origins in the ancient Tuscan dialect.
5. the language
6. to speak properly
7. They do not want to make love.
8. with all of them like this
9. in mind
10. I could stay here, it could be a permanent place for me. These women would be good wives.

16ª Le Napoletane
Simpatiche è brune
Con scarse Scuaglione
Che fanno in Cartari
Dei bei Costumi
Mangiate anche ture
Di alta natura
Nel far l'amore
Andando per via
Vi fanno l'occhietto
E il cuor dal petto
Vi fanno Balzare
Ok diamo alla punta
Del gran stivale
Se non vi fa male
Ancor ascoltar.
17ª Dirrò che le donne
Che san Calabrese

16a Le Napoletane	16a The women of Naples
Simpatiche è brune	They are very nice with dark hair/skin
Con scarle scuaglione[1]	with scarce sweaters
Che fanno in cadar[2]	Made with wool
Dei bei costume[3]	They wear beautiful costumes
Mangiate andature	The way they eat and the way they walk / move about
Di alta natura	Is a higher class
Nel far l'amore	in making love
Andavano per via[4]	When they walk by you
Vi fanno l'occhietto	They wink at you
E il cuoro dal petto[5]	It makes your heart jump in your chest
Vi fanno balzar	They make you leap
Or siamo all punta	now we are at the tip
Del gran stivale[6]	of a big boot
Se non vi fa male	It does not hurt you
Ancor ascoltar[7]	to continue to listen
17a Dirrò che le donne	17a I will say that the women
Che son Calabrese	that are Calabrian

Author Commentary

1. rarely found sweaters
2. cadar is a type of expensive wool
3. clothes
4. on the street
5. skip a beat with excitement
6. He wishes he was in Rome or Naples seducing one of those beautiful women, or searching for a wife. It is bad enough that he and his fellow captives were betrayed by their own country. Now they are the tip of a metaphorical Austrian boot in the ass on a daily basis.
7. to my commentary on the women of the world.

Continued on pg 123

son poco cortese
con gente straniera
Esse amano troppo
La patria sonstanza
perché n'anno abastanza
Di fulame così...
18 Le Siciliane
Di sangue bollente
D'aspetto attraente
Fedeli in amor,
con chi si avvicinano
Non sono troppo leste
Ma per chi le conosce
Ne staranno a sentir
Ad abbandonarle
con nessuna Consiglio
Le occulte sparmiglie
Vi sanno mostrar

Son poco cortese	are not very courteous.
Con gente stranier	with people they don't know
Esse amino troppo	They have too much love
La patria sonstanza[8]	???????
Perchè ne'anno abastanza	?????????Because they have enough
Di sulame cosi	?????????Of salami like this
18a Le Siciliane	18a The Sicilian women
Di sangue bollente	with hot blood
D'aspetto attranta	They are beautiful
Fedeli in Amor	Faithful in love
Con chi si avvicinano	with the people they are close to
Non sono troppo leste	They are not very fast to interact with you
Ma per che le conosce	But for those who they know
Ne staranno a sentir	They will listen.
Ad abbandonarle	To leave / abandon them
Con nessuna consiglio	I don't suggest to anyone.
Le occute sparniglie	?????
Vi sanno mostrar[9]	They will show you

8. These three lines are nearly impossible to interpret.   *continued from page 121*

9. They will have revenge

Per quanto ne ho veduto
Nel mondo passato
Come la bruzzese
Ne dunna ho trovato
son troppo vergognose
non si lasciano toccare
Mai sola la lasciano
Per poterci parlar
Se la fortuna ti viene
di sola trovarla
sei sicuro di toccarla
Di dentro e di fuori
Ed ora Signori
Mi turo la Bocca
La mia filistocca
Vi voglio finir.
Gia troppo mi pare
Di troppo seccardi

Per quanto ne ho veduto	I have seen a lot of things
Nel mondo passato	In the past
Come la bruzzese	Those from Aburzzo
Ne sunna ho trovato¹	I found none of them
Son troppos vergogniose	they are shy
Non si lasciano toccare	They don't let you touch them.
Mai sola la lasciano²	They are never left alone
Per poterci parlar	For you to be able to speak to them
Le la fortuna ti viene	You would have to be lucky
Di sola trovarla	to find her by herself.
Si sicuro di toccarla	You are sure to touch her
Di dentro e di fuori³	on the inside and the outside.
Ed ora signori	and now gentlemen
Mi turo la bocca	I shut my mouth
La mia filistocca	My little poem
Vi voglio fimir.	I want to end.
Gia troppo mi pare	I think it is too much
Di troppo seccarvi⁴	It gets dry

Author Commentary

1. I never met one of them
2. The women are always supervised.
3. Touch her heart and body
4. I am boring you too much

Non voglio annoiarvi
Con questa canzon
Ma se v'e gradito
Battete le mani
Che il resto domani
Vi faccio sentir.

Fine Godiny
il 26/12/1917

Fame in Austria

Non Voglioannoiarvi	I don't want to bore you
Con quest canzon	with this song/poem
Ma se vi e Gradito	but if you welcome/appreciate it
Battele le mani	Clap your hands
Che il resto domani	Then the rest tomorrow
Vi faccio sentir	I will let you know.
Fine Goding	The end Goding
il 24/12/1917	24/12/1917
Fame in Austria	Hunger in Austria

Author Commentary

1. to be continued

Figure 48: Sleeping in the trenches

Orfanelle senza tetto
da Gorizia siam venute
senza pane e senza letto
fin le vesti abbiam perdute,
Non abbiamo il caro padre
Non abbiamo più una madre
Che di noi si prenda cuor.
2ª Sotto il Rombo del cannone
siam vissute mesi e mesi
Con nel cor Trepidazione
Molti giorni abbiam presi
A pregar nelle cantine
Se le spalle si videro
Ci scuotevan di terror.
3ª Quanto è dura nostra sorte
Noi vedemmo in questa guerra
Fuoco, orror rovina e morte
Passeggiar su nostra terra!
Nell'immane ria sciagura
E di tal maggior sventura
Ci fu detto di partir

Orfanella Sensa Tetto[1]

"Il Pregar dell'Orfanella Sale a Dio"

Da Gorizia siam venute

Senza pane e senza letto

Fin le vesti abbiam perdute,

Non abbiamo il caro padre

Non abbiamo più una madre

Che di noi si prenda cuor.

2a Sotto il rombo del cannone

Siam vissute mesi e mesi

con nel cor trepidazione

Molti giorni abbiamo spese

A preg nelle cantine[2]

Ve le spalle si vicine

Ci scuotevan di terror

3a Quanto è dura nostro sorte

Noi Vedemmo in questa Guerra

Fuoco, orror rovina e morte

passeggiar su nostra terra!

Nell'immane sia sciaguro

A evitar maggior sventura

Ci fu detto di partir[3]

Orphan Without a Roof

"The Prayer of the Orphan Rises up to God"

We have come from Gorizia.

Without bread and without a bed.

Without the clothes that we have lost.

We do not have a dear father.

We no longer have a mother

To take care of us.

2a Under the roar of the cannons

We have lived for months and months

with trepidation in our hearts.

Many days we have spent in

In prayer in the cellar.

We were shoulder to shoulder.

We were shocked with terror.

3a How hard is our fate

We saw in this war

Fire, horror, ruin and death

walking on our land!

In the terrible misfortune

To avoid greater misfortune

They told us to depart.[4]

Author Commentary

1. A Homeless Orphan
2. Underground or in the trenches.
3. Now that the battle has destroyed the town of Gorizia, we have orders to march to another town and bring horror, ruin, and death to it as well

Continued on pg 130

4ª Eccellenza, quanto è dura
Questa vita dell'esiglio
Bene è ver che questa mano
Rasciugarono sul ciglio
L'omai lungo nostro pianto
E una buona madre intanto
Ci teneste il gran martìre
5 Grazie a voi, benefattori!
Il pregar dell'orfanella
Sale a Dio; i suoi tesori
All'umile sua favella
Su voi chiamano e lunga vita,
Poi la grazia più sentita
Della gioia senza fin!
6ª Ma il lor grazie più amoroso,
Il lor grazie singolare,
Il lor grazie rispettoso
Vengon a voi che di speciale
Zelo avete, e gran clemenza
Al curare, o Eccellenza,
D'orfanelle il pio destin
Le orfanelle profu... dell'istituto

continued from page 129

4. At this point his poem becomes a humble and fervent prayer to His Excellence, Jesus Christ. He prays to the great martyr for delivery from the fire, horror, and death that surrounds him. Fedele's Catholic faith was well-established before the war. He

130

4a Eccellenza, quanta è dura
quest vita dell'esiglio
Ria scingurano sul esiglio[5]
L'omai lungo nostro pianto[6]
E una buona madre intanto
Ci lensisce il gran martire[7]
5a Grazi a voi, benefattori!
Il pregar dell'orfanella
sale a Dio, I suoi tesor
Nell'umile sua favella
su voi chiama e lunga vita,[8] per la grazia piu sentitia
Della gioia senza fin!
6a Ma il loro grazie più amoroso
Il lor grazie singolare,
Il lor grazie rispettoso
Vengo a voi che si speciale
Zelo avete, e gran clemenza
Nel Curare, o Eccellenza,
D'orfanelle il mio destin
Le orfanelle fra fu istituto
Conto dalle di Gorizia.

4a Excellence, how hard is it
this life of the exile?
They were on the edge.
By now our crying is long
And a good mother in time
Great martyr, relieve us the pain.
5a Thanks to you, benefactors!
The prayer of the orphan
rises up to you God, in your treasures.
In her humble prayer
she calls upon you for a long life.
but the most heartfelt grace is
Of the joy without end!
6a But their most loving thanks
Their singular thanks
My respectful thanks
I send to you, who are so special
You have great clemency.
We are in the care of our benevolent God.
To be an orphan is my destiny.
The orphan from the institute
Song of those from Gorizia.

---

draws the strength to live through his faith in God. The Austrians want to kill him; he is hungry, tired, and scared, He is going from one battle to another, while living in the dirt. Just like a homeless orphan, faith in God, and the will to live is all he can rely on.

5. Perhaps he means the edge between life and death
6. our suffering is prolonged
7. Jesus was the greatest martyr
8. the orphan

[Handwritten letter in Italian cursive script, dated Dicembre 24, 1917]

Dalle memorie d'un Prigioniero Dicembre 24 1917

Eccoci alla vigilia del Santo natale... Siamo ancora in cinque compagnia. Il nostro pensiero vola come sempre alle lontane Famiglie, e con tutta la nostalgia del passato ci sembra vedere le nostre care mamme tutte affaccendate, a preparare e pulire ad adornare la nostra modesta casa. I bambini nella loro innocenza trastullano, e giubilando cantano lode al Bambino Gesù, che da esso attendano i doni che tanto desiderano. Cari ricordi della nostra infanzia, le Campane squillano melodicamente e le dolci note tengono fisso il pensiero che Domani e la gran Tradizionale festa del Rendentor Gesù, così ci sembra e tale era prima di questa sciagurata guerra. Questa all'usione e' breve. Poichè subito si viene alla realtà, e' scompare ogni sentimento gaio, e con angoscia vediamo le nostre brave mamme.

Author Commentary

1. Here we are, it is Christmas eve. Here we are with five companions.
2. In Italy, the Christmas morning gifts are not from Santa Clause. They are brought by the baby Jesus.
3. The Loria home on Via Vallone was only a few yards from the family church, Santa Maria della Grazia, Holy Mary of Grace. He would have heard the bells in the tower

Dalle memoreie di un Prigioniero
Dicebre 24, 1917

"I bambini nella loro innocenza trastullano e giutivi cantano lode al Bambino Jesù"

Eccoci alla vigilia del Santo natale . . . Siamo a . . . in Cinque compagni.[1]

Il nostro pensiero vola come semper alle lontane famiglie

e con tutta la nostalgia del passato ch sembra vedere le nostre

mamme tutte affaccendate, a preparare a pulire ad adornare la nostra modesto casa.

I bambini nella loro innocenza trastullano e giutivi cantano lode al Bambino Jesù

che da esso attemdano I doni che tanto desideranno.[2]

Cari ricordi della nostra infanzia le campane squilano melodicamente

e le dolci note tengono fisso il pensiero che domani e la gran tradizionale festa del Rendetor Jesu[3]

Cosi ci sembra e tale era prima di questa sgiagurata gerra.

Questa all'usione è breve poichè subito si vieni alla realtà è scompare ogni sentiment gaio e con angoscia[4]

Vediamo le nostre brave mamme,

From the Memories of a Prisoner
December 24, 1917

"Children in Their Innocence Playing and Coming Together Singing Praises to Baby Jesus"

We are here, it is the vigil of Holy Christmas.

Our thoughts fly as usual to the far away families,

with all the nostalgia of the past. It seems to us that we see our dear

mothers busy getting ready to prepare and clean and decorate our modest homes.

The little children in their innocence playing and coming together singing praises to baby Jesus.

They are anticipating from Him the gifts that they so desire.

Dear warm memories of our childhood, the bells of the church ringing melodically

and the sweet notes keep fixed the thought that tomorrow is the great tradi—tional festival of the savior Jesus.

It seems to us it was like this before this wretched war.

This illusion is brief because immediately one comes to the reality and every senti—ment of joy with anguish.

We see our good/brave mothers,

ringing hundreds of times, every Sunday, every important feast day, Easter, and of course Christmas Eve and Christmas mornings. No doubt the memory of those bells could, at least temporarily, transfix his thoughts on his childhood, his home, and his mother, that he may never see again.

4. The literal translation does not work well here. It would make more sense to say that "immediately one comes to reality, and every sentiment of joy is replaced with anguish."

133

tristi e pensierose che attendano alle loro faccende, ma
non tranquille, ma non felici. E vagano col
pensiero lontano. Ci sembra di vederle muovere e
rimuovere oggetti senza mai riuscire ad assentire
come vorrebbero, e come solevano quando il loro cuore
non era ferito, quando il loro spirito era tranquillo!...
Povere mamme! Come noi a loro il loro pensiero
è là presso i loro amati figli. E li vedono costretti
nel fango della trincea, sofferenti, intirizziti dal
freddo. Li immaginano nel terribile momento
dell'assalto, e prima di muovere il passo verso
il nemico volgere il pensiero a loro, inviar un saluto
un bacio che è l'ultimo e poi con impeto slanciarsi tra
fragore dei cannoni, tra il sinistro rumore della
mitragliatrice, tra la grandine dei proiettili al
grido della folla, o poco dopo cadere rantolanti, e
con voce fioca... mamma... muoio... addio...
t'aspetto lassù. Li vedono nel letto

tristi e pensieroseche attendano loro faccenede

sad and pensive as they do their housework,

Ma non tranquille, ma non felici. E vagano colpensiero lontano,[1]

Not at peace and not happy. They wander around with their thoughts far away.

Ci Sembra Di Vederle nuovere e rimovere oggetti sensa mai riuscire ad assentare[2]

It seems to us that we see them moving and moving again, objects without ever getting them.

Come vorebbero e come solevano quando il loro cuore non era ferito[3].

The way they used to be before when their hearts were not wounded.

Quando il loro spirito era tranquillo! . . . Povere mamme!

When their spirit was peaceful! . . . Poor mothers!

Come noi a loro il loro pensiero è la presso / loro amati figli.[4]

It is like that from us to them, in the same way that their thoughts go to their beloved sons.

E li vedono costretti nel fango della trincea sofferenti, in tirizitti dal freddo[5]

And they see us forced into the mud of the trenches suffering and shut up from the cold.

Li immaginano nel terribile momento dell'assalto, è prima di muovere[6]

They imagine us in the terrible moments just before we move in assault.

Il passo verso il nemico volgere il pensiero a loro, inviar un salute un bacio che

In the advance towards the enemy their thoughts turn to us, they send out wishes for our health and send us a kiss

È l'ultimo e pi con impero slaciarsi tra fragore dei cannoni;

It is the last one, then we throw ourselves between the roar of the cannons

tra il sinistro rumore della mitrgliatrice, tra la grandne dei provettili between

the sinister roar of the machine guns and the hail of bullets

al grido della folia, of poco dopo cadere ranttolanti,e con voce fiocca . . .

And the crazy shouting, after a few moments falling and gasping he fell back, and with a soft voice . . .

Mamma. . . .Mmuoio. . . Adio. . . T'aspetto lassu[7]

Mamma . . . I am dying . . . I wait for you up there.

Continued on pg 136

Author Commentary

1. They wander around as if they are lost
2. They see their mothers absently mindedly wandering around the house fussing and fiddling around with household chores

continued from page 135

3. Knowing that your son is in a concentration camp as a prisoner of war certainly would cause a mother's heart to ache.

4. The thoughts are mutual between mothers and sons. As the mothers constantly worry about their sons, the sons are concerned about their mother's aching hearts and worried minds. Under circumstances like this, there is little a mother can do except worry. But there was one thing she could do. She could send packages to her son. He wrote of sixteen packages from home. The family was poor, but I'm sure she thought, "My son is a prisoner of war, cost be dammed." I know she poured her heart into each of those packages, Fedele specifically says he received shoes, pants, sweaters, and underwear from home. We don't know what else his mother sent to him. It is likely she would have included dried sausages, cheeses, and other foods, medicine, a warm hat, blankets, some personal hygiene items, perhaps even a blank diary book, a quill pen, and ink. It is unlikely that she could read or write. Perhaps she had a literate friend who could include an encouraging note in the box. In the Mauthausen concentration camp, death from exposure, disease, beatings, and starvation was a daily occurrence. In a cold climate, a man needs about 3,000 calories daily for good health. The average POW in Austria was receiving about 1,000 calories in daily rations. It is not unreasonable to say that his mother is the reason he survived. So many details are lost to time. If only we could talk to them now. The Red Cross facilitated the delivery of packages to prison camps in Austria. Later in the diary, Fedele records eight packages received from the Red Cross.

5. Shut up from the cold could mean their lips were so cold they could not speak.

6. The mothers realize that their sons would be sick with terror just before stepping in front of a machine gun.

7. a final goodbye

Postcard of prisoner Corriani at Goding. 1 July 1917.

"Memory of our imprisonment in Goding
Greetings and kisses."

Figure 49: Postcard of prisoner Corriani

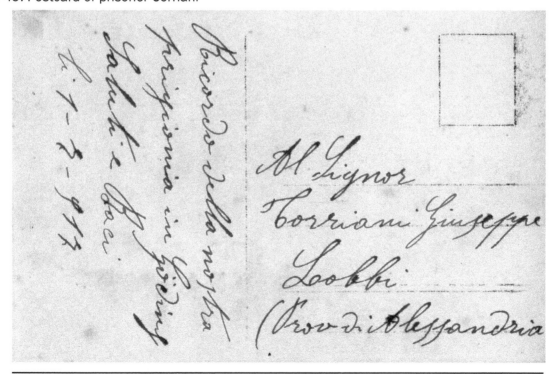

Figure 50: Reverse of postcard of prisoner Corriani

dell'ospedale che soffriamo di ferite, e le buone
suore prestar loro le cure necessarie, e loro non
riconoscere la necessità, da esse e chiamare mamma
è la mamma, che deve guarirle; la sua parola e il suo
affetto, e la medicina che cercano e che sembra si
guarisca.. Li immaginano giacenti al suolo feriti
pridiosi, ecco di, invocando aiuto chiamare
il dolce nome. Li imaginano Prigionieri del
nemico. stanchi, freddoli, affamati, chiedere
un pozzo di mare il quale viene loro negato
e il soldato di scorta scorta con rudibi mochigli
spinge avanti e loro umiliati gli abbassare il cappe
e con gli occhi in pianto trascinarsi faticosame
te, mamme e troppo il vostro dolore, lo
immaginiamo, il cuore vi si strazio, e nulla
potete fare per i vostri amati se non con
la vostra fervida prece a Dio attingere
conforto e speranza ...

Ci vedono nel letto dell' ospedale che soffriamo di ferrite e le buone suore prestar loro le cure neccessarie,

They see us in the hospital bed wounded and suffering, and the good nuns give us the necessary cure

e loro non riconscre la neccessità, da esse e chiamare mamma

and they don't understand the need to call out mamma.

E la mamma, che deve guarire; la sua parola e il suo affetto, e la medicina che cercano e che sembra li guarisco.

It is the mother that must give the cure. Her words and her affection is the medicine that they are searching for to get well.

Ci immaginano gia centi al suolo feriti

They imagine us already on the ground wounded.

Prividi, secco ti invocando aiuto chiamare il doce nome.[1]

Cold and malnourished invoking help and calling the sweet name. (Of their mother)

Ci imaginano prigioniere de nemico. Anchi, freddi, affamati, chiedere un pozzo

They imagine us as prisoners of the enemy, also cold, hungry, asking for a piece

Di mare il quale viene loro negato e il soldato di scorta con runvidi modi gli spinge avanti

of dried fish that is denied to them. The guards in a rough manner push you forward.

E loro umiliati abbassare il cappo e con gli occhi in pianio trascinarsi

They are humiliated with head lowered and tears in the eyes, they are dragged along

faticosamente, mamme e troppo il vostro dolore, lo immaginiamo il cuore di si strazio,

difficultly, mothers your pain is too much, we imagine your heart is tormented

e nulla potete fare per i vostri amati, se non con la vostra fervida prece a dio

there is nothing you can do for your loved ones, except with your fervent prayers to God

attingere comfort e Speranza . . .

to draw comfort and hope . . .

AUTHOR'S NOTE

The date is Christmas Eve, 1917. Normally this would be a happy day at home with family. The nostalgic feelings of joy he might have felt fade as the sun sets. Perhaps this was a day when all seemed lost. How could he not be depressed when so many things were against him? He felt betrayed by his country because the Italian government blocked lifesaving packages from home and the Red Cross. For months he ate nothing but dried fish and fava beans. He watched other prisoners die from starvation, exhaustion, disease, and exposure. Fedele was in hell on earth. In "The Taking of Black Mountain," he writes, "betrayed by my own country." He was, in fact, betrayed and abandoned by the country that he loved. He volunteered to join the army and was willing to die for his fatherland. He did not surrender at the battle of Caporetto. He was wounded, then captured while unconscious. Later, his country abandoned him in prison. After all, he had been through, how could he not feel that his country was the tip of the boot that had kicked him and left him to die?

The winter weather in the Austrian Alps is brutal. He was underfed, lacking proper clothing, behind barbed wire, under armed guard, and living with the very real threat of beating, or worse, every day. He knew his mother's heart was breaking with grief and worry. She had two more very good reasons to worry. Her other sons, Giovanni and Antonio, were also away at war. We do not know where they were during the war, but they did survive. Few of us have been in circumstances that were this sad and depressing. Experiences like this will shape a man's life and leave marks on his soul that last a lifetime.

Fedele's love for his family burns brightly in the darkness of this night. His daughters, Mafalda, Genevieve, Margarite, Mary, and his grandchildren emphasized to me that he had an immense love for his family. He showed this love throughout his entire lifetime in the form of examples of how to be a good father, husband, friend, and provider. For most of his adult life, he had two of the most dangerous jobs in the world. The first was an infantryman in the trenches and a prisoner of war. The second was mining coal. Coal mining was difficult by any measure. Maybe mining did not seem quite so bad compared to what he lived through in the winter of 1917–1918. In the first job, he sacrificed for his country. Then he did what he had to do for love of family.

Postcard of prisoner Distefano at Goding. 2 July 1917.

"Memory of our imprisonment in Goding
Greetings and kisses."

Figure 51: Postcard of prisoner Distefano

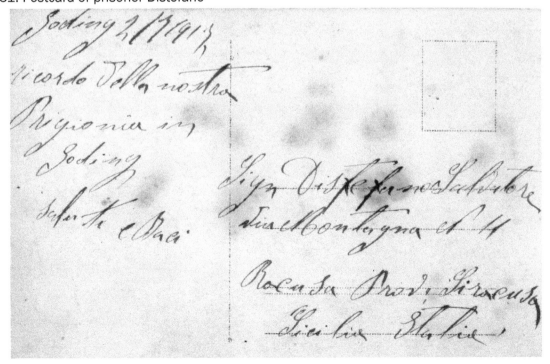

Figure 52: Reverse postcard of prisoner Distefano.

Il giorno che io vorrei essere gaio, tristamente
si oscura e si indora la sera. Allora più
triste ancora vola il vostro pensiero e fisso
sempre alla lontana nostra patria vediamo nel
focolare domestico di case romite la mamma, che
col rosario tra le mani mestamente prega
rompendo ogni tanto il nostro triste silenzio
con qualche sfuggito singhiozzo. Il vecchio padre
seduto al tavolo guardando dalla parte opposta dove
siede la sua amata vecchietta per non far scorgere
la tristezza del suo volto colla sua testa
appoggiata ad una mano, collo sguardo fisso
nell'ombra guardar lontano, ogni tanto senza farse
accorgere si asciuga una lagrima che malgrado la
sua volontà di tenersi— fastidiamente gli
scorre lungo la guancia. In un altro canto
al mio scanto seduta si nesta la giovine sposa
tenendo sulle ginocchia il suo fanciulletto che

Il giorno che io vrebbe essere gaio, tristamente si oscura e si inolerla sera.

> The day I would like to be happy, sadly it darkens and fades away in the evening.

Allora piu triste ancora si la il nostro pensiero e fisso sempre alla lontana nostra patria'

> Then it is even more sad as our thoughts are fixed always on our far away fatherland

Vediamo nel focolare domestic di case romite? la mamma, che col rosario tra le mani

> We see in our fireplaces at home(s)? the mother with a rosary in their hands

Mesfamente prega rompendo ogni tanto il nostro triste silenzio con qualche sfuggitio singhiozzo.

> with sadness praying, occasionally breaking our sad silence with some quiet sobs.

Il Vecchio padre seduto al tavolo quardando dall parte oppost di sieda la sua amata vecchietta

> The aged father sitting at the table look—ing in the direction away from where his beloved wife sits

per non far sporgere la tristeza del suo volto colla sua testa appoggia tra ad una mano,

> so as not to let her see the sadness of his face with his shoulders and his head in his hand

collo squardo fisso che sembra guardar lontano,

> he doesn't move, and he appears to stare at something far away.

Ogni tanto senza farlo scorgere si ascingua una lagrima che mal grado la sua volontà

> Occasionally without trying he has a tear against his will.

Di tenersi fortivamente gli scorre lungo la guancia.

> He tries to control himself, but the tears flow strongly down his cheeks.

In un altro canto il mio scuro seduta se ne sta fu giovine sposa[2]

> In a different semi dark corner the young bride is seated

Tenendo sulle ginocchia il suo fanciuletto che.

> She holds on her knee a little boy that

Author Commentary

1. homes
2. in a dark corner

appena balbetta qualche parolae... mamma, gli disse.
Viene il Bambino e il Papà perché non viene a casa?
A tale innocente domanda alla giovane si
riempono gli occhi di lagrime, e trattenendo con
fatica il pianto, segna col dito al suo Bambino:
Il Papà è lassù.
Poveri genitori; Povera sposa! È annuncio
d'ipochi o più giorni che il suo amato è caduto
combattendo, le ha schiantato il cuore, come
un fulmine colpendo schianta un rigoglioso
Albero...
La gioia la tranquillità, la pace nell'affetto famigliare di un tempo, nella ricorrenza
di questi giorni, s'è invertito in dolore in
pianto e in disperazione.
La voce vibrata di un compagno che è sempre
il più allegro ci scuote da questo letargo che
ci teneva assopiti esclamando:

appena balbetta qalche parole gli disse: Viene il bambino e il papa perchè non viene a casa?

can babble only a few words. The little boy said, "Where is daddy, why does he not come home?"

A tale innocente domanda all giovane si riempono gli occhi di lagrime

At this innocent question the young woman's eyes fill with tears.

Trattenendo con fu lca? il pianto, segna col dito al suo bambino il papà e lassù

Holding back the tears she points with her finger that your father is up there.

Poveri genitore, povera sposa! `E annuncio di pochi o più giorni che il suo amato è caduto

Poor parents, poor bride! It was announced only a few days ago that her beloved is fallen.

Combattendo, le ha schianta o il cuore, come un fulmine colpendo schianta un rigoglioso albero . . .

She was stricken in her heart, just as if a lighting had struck a tree

La gioia la tranquililità, la pace nell affetto famigliare di un tempo, nella ricorrenza di questi

The joy, the tranquility, the peace in the family affection from a time passed

Giorni se inventò in dolore in pianto e in disperanzione

In these days invents the pain and tears and desperation.

La voce vibrata di un compagno che è semper il più allegro che scuote da questo letargo¹

The shaky voice of a friend that among us is usually the happiest among us astonishes us in this hibernation

Ci teneva assopiti esclamandó

That keeps us dormant.

Author Commentary

1. lethargy
2. A literal translation here is easy to do, but difficult to understand. I have the impression that this sad scene, as he imagines it, is not of just one home, but it has occurred in thousands of households across Europe that have had the lightning strike. Before the war, the families had peace, tranquility, and affection among themselves. Their lives, their peace and tranquility, was brutally shattered, as in when lighting explodes inside a tree. When their beloved son/husband dies, then it becomes exquisitely painful to mourn the loss of the one who brought tranquility, peace, and affection into their home. Quiet desperation fills their hearts, and their days, as they settle into the shock. Fedele knew many that died. Some of those deaths would have caused the kind of pain that he describes. He feels compassion for the families so deeply that he is compelled to pour out the feelings in his heart onto paper. More than once, he tells us he fears death. It would not surprise me if he feared the possibility of this shock for his mother and siblings more than he feared death itself.

Oh corpo di tutti i diavoli, che facciamo qui tutti ammutoliti come tanti frati nelle loro meditazioni? Dobbiamo svegliarsi e dare bando a tutte fandonie e pensieri chi ci vogliono impiccare.

Via tutte le piagnucolerie e pensiamo che domani è il giorno che è nato il Redentore ad ogni costo lo dobbiamo distinguere coll'essere anche noi più allegri. Vadano alla malora anche quei quattro quattrini che teniamo imprigionati nel Borsellino. Tante cose dobbiamo fare! Rimetterci a questa vita non possiamo, e nemmeno per i nostri compagni che son morti e per quelli che van là ad ammazzire nelle trincee. Anche noi abbiamo fatto la nostra parte e.... Il diavolo non ci ha voluti; quindi è segno che dobbiamo vivere ancora e per vivere un po' tranquilli bisogna farsi forti e dimenticare il passato e il.... presente.

Oh corpo di tutti I diavoli,

"e non pensareci al future anzisi pensareci ma per stare alegri."

Oh body of all the devils.

"Don't think of the future and try to be happy."

Oh corpo di tutti I diavoli'

che facciamo qui tutti ammuto li ti come tanti frati nele loro mediazioni?

Dobbiamo svegliarsi e dare bando at tutte fandonie e pensieri chi ci vogliono inforcure

Via tutte le piagnuscolerie e pensiamo che domani è il giorno che è nato

Il Rendetore ad ogni costo lo dobbiamo distiguere coll'essere anch noi piu allegri'

Va dano alla ma lora anche quei quatro quatrini che tenniamo imprigionati nel borselino,

Tant cose dobbiamo Fare!

Rimediarci a questa vita non possiamo e nemeno per i nostri compagni che son morti e per quelli che son la'ad ammufire nelle trincee

Anche noi abbiamo fatto la nostra parte è . . .

Il diavolo non ci ha voluti quinid è segno che

Dobbiamo vivere ancora e per vivere un p'o tranquilly bisogna farsi forti e dimenticare il passato

E il . . . . Presente

Oh body of all the devils.

What are we doing here mute, as if we are so many friars/priests in meditation?

We must wake ourselves and banish all the lies and thoughts of those who want us kill us.

Away with all the whining and let's think of tomorrow that is the day of birth

Of the Savior, at every cost we must do everything in our power to be a little happier

We must give those four pennies that we keep imprisoned here in our little purse.

There are a lot of things we must do!

We cannot remedy this life at least for our friends who are dead and for those that are rotting in the trenches.

We have done our part . . .

The devil did not want us, so it is a sign that

We must continue to live, and live more peacefully, we must be strong and forget the past

and live in the present

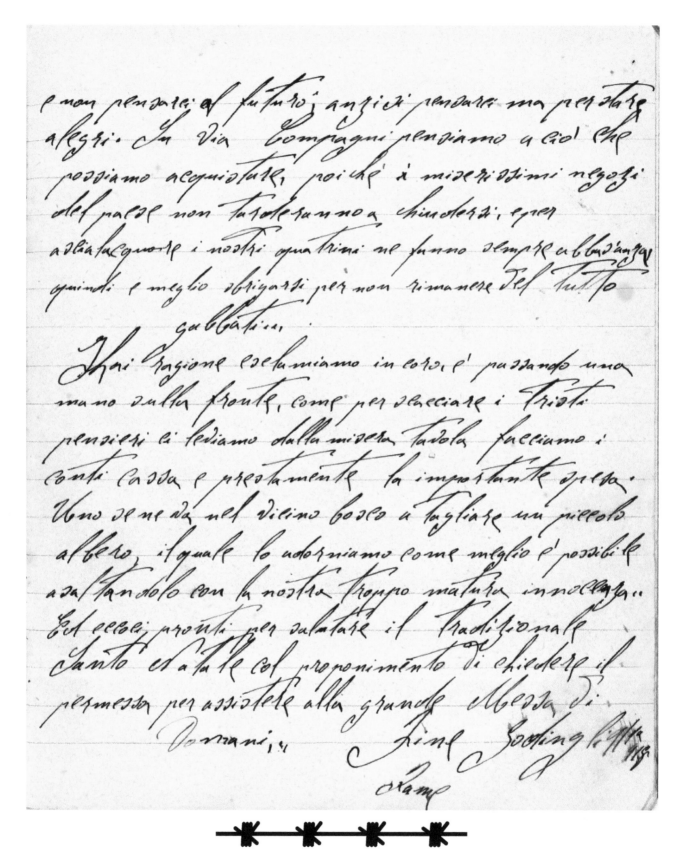

Author Commentary

1. Fedele's attitude on this Christmas Eve is a real mix of sarcasm, positive attitude, and pragmatism. Essentially, he says: Why are we sitting around in sad silence like monks

e non pensareci al futuro anzisi pensareci ma per stare alegri.

don't think of the future, and try to be happy.

La mia compagni pensiamo acquistare, poichè I miserissimi negozi del paese

My friends let's think of the things we can acquire, because the miserable shops

del paese non tarderanno a chiuderesi a scialcquore I nostril quatrini ne fanno

in this area will soon be closing before we can squander our money. They will be enough

Quindi e meglio sbringarsi per non rimanere del tutto gabbi

So it is better to hurry so as not to be completely cheated.

Hai ragione esclamiamo in coro,è passando una mano sulla fronte, come per scacciare I triste

You are right we exclaim in chorus, pass—ing a hand on the forehead, as if to drive away the sad

pensieri ci leviamo dall misera tavola facciamo I conti cassa e prestamente la importante spesa.

thoughts. Let's get up from this miserable/poor table and count our money and do important shopping.

Uno se ne va nel vicino bosca a tagliare un piccolo albero, il quale lo adorniamo come

One of us should go into the nearby forest and cut down a small tree. We will decorate it as

Meglio è possible. A saltandolo con la nostra troppo matura innocenza.[2]

As best as we can. We will jump over it with our mature innocence

Ed eccolci pronti per salutare il tradizionale Santo Natale col proponimento di chiedere

And now we are here ready to greet the traditional Holy Christmas day with intention of asking

Permessa per assistere all grande Messa di Domani.[3]

For permission to assist in the high Mass of

Fine Goding 24/12/1917

Tomorrow.

The end Goding 24 December 1917

Fame

Hunger

meditating on the past? Think of your bright future here in prison, be happy. Keep your chins up fellows. Remember, the devil didn't want us, we were not good enough for hell. We are alive, let's keep living for our friends who are dead, or are still in the trenches. We have only four pennies among us. The miserable shops in this prison will close soon, so let's go Christmas shopping!

2. His sarcasm shines here. Just as if they can just walk out of prison carrying an ax to cut down a Christmas tree. Then we will decorate it and jump over it in a game as if we are little kids.

3. His fantasy in sarcasm comes back to reality. Tomorrow is Christmas day, and he must ask the guards for permission to go to mass.

Italiano	Tedesco
Preciso o puntuale -	Bestim
Dove va	To cher si ein « Vou
Cosa vuoi	Vas vollen -
Cosa hai fatto	Vas ausi gemackt
Mi vuole lei bene	Haus mich gorne
Io la amo di molto	Ich liebe sufil
Come si chiama il suo nome	Ti haise si vi nam
Dove andaste	To varen si
Oggi mi ha fatto arrabiare -	Aite ausi mir per
Cosa ha fatto ieri -	Vas haw si gestern gemach
Io mi chiamo -	Ich aise
Brutto	Silin
Ridere	Lachen

Practicing German Vocabulary

FEDELE'S ABILITY TO write in German was extremely limited. He heard the words in German, but he wrote them as he would say them with his Italian accent. Many Italian words end with the letter "i," and so do many of *his* German words. There are *no* German words that end with the letter "i." Therefore, nearly every German word is misspelled. On the bottom of that page, he practices his signature.

On the diary page, you see this practice vocabulary in its entirety, with the Italian and German words. I have provided you with only the English translation.

Italian translated to English:

Italiano Italian	Tedesco (German)
Presiso o punctuale	Precise or punctual
Dove va	Where are you going?
Cosa Vuoi	What do you want?
Cosa hai fatto	What have you done?
Mi vuole lei bene	She cares for me
Io la amo di molto	I love you a lot
Come si chiama il suo nome	What is your name?
Dove andatte	Where are you going?
Oggi mi ha fatto arrabiare	Today you made me angry
Cosa ha fatto Ieri	What did he do yesterday?
Io mi chiamo	My name is
Brutto	ugly
Ridere	laugh

151

Evidenza

Centrale dei pacchi Sigmundsherberg

Göding 2/3/1918

Le nostre Famiglie costantemente inviano delle Cartoline colla quale giustificano la spedizione dei pacchi noi non sappiamo a quale causa si possa attribuirne fatto sta che da 7 mesi non ricevo nulla. Quindi si rivolgiamo a Codesto comando dei pacchi in Sigmundsherberg affinché voglia vivamente interessarsi Ringraziandovi Anticipatamente Saluti.

Loria Fedele N° 41925 Campo di Concentramento Mauthausen

Presso Baumeister Anton Müller

Tabak Fabrich Göding Mähren

V. Martino Giovanni Kukuck Gusztáv

Veahi

Porsongmegze,

Vi Martino Giovanni

Evidenza Centrale dei Pacchi Sigmundsherberg Goding 2/7 1918

Le nostre famiglie costantemente ci inviano

delle cartoline colla quale giustificano la spedizoine dei pacchi.[1]

Noi non sappiamo a quale causa si possa attribuir ne fatto sta che da 7 mesi non ricevo nulla.

si rivolgiamo a codesto

Dei pacchi in Sigmundsherberg affinche voglia vivamente interessarsi

Ringraziamdo vi anticipatamente salute.

Loria Fedele N° 41925 Campo di

Concentramento Mauthausen

Presso Baumaeister[2]

Evidence of the Parcels from Sigmundsherberg Goding 2 July 1918

Our families are constantly sending us

post cards which verify the shipment of packages.

We don't know for what reason one can attribute the fact that for 7 months I have received nothing.

So, we call on this office

Of the packages in Sigmundsherberg so that you may want to take an interest.

We thank you in advance, goodby.

Loria Fedele N° 41925 Camp

Concentration Mauthausen

At Baumaeister

Author Commentary

1. to us
2. Fedele is painfully aware that he and his fellow prisoners have packages that should have been delivered to them. The Austrians used the nearby Sigmundsherburg concentration camp as a central location to hold the packages. He doesn't know why these essential packages of food and clothing are delayed. In frustration, and with a lot of sarcasm, he pretends to write a letter to Central Packaging, at Sigmundsherburg. He finishes the letter with his full return address and signatures of several of his fellow prisoners.

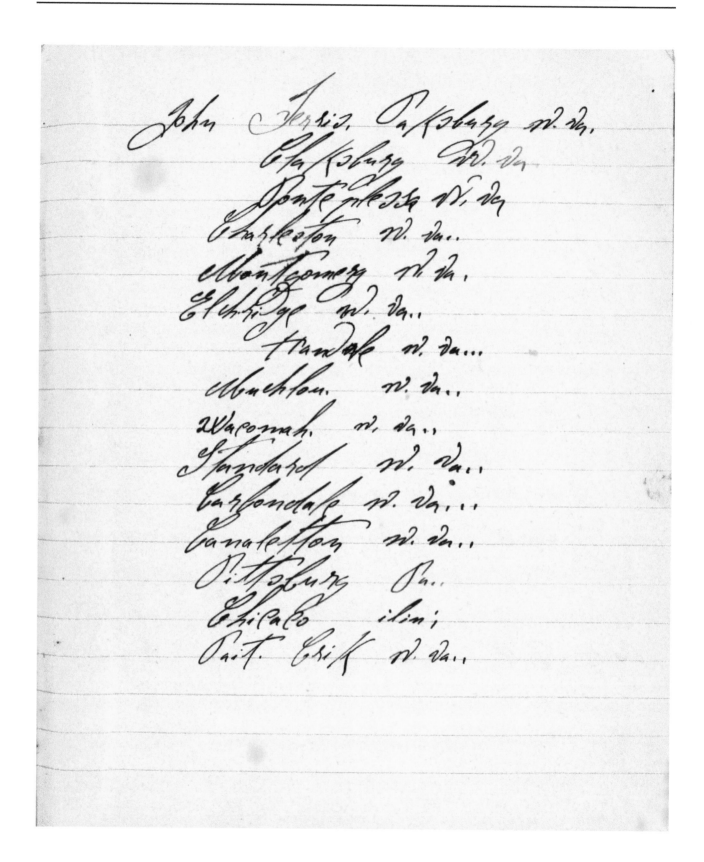

Practicing Names of American Towns

FEDELE PRACTICES WRITING names of towns in America. Most of these places are small mining villages. A few of these towns were close to where he lived, in Boomer or Logan, West Virginia.

John Ferris, Paksburg W. Va.	Parkersburg
Clarksburg W. Va.	Clarksburg W. Va.
Ponte Plessa W. Va.	Point Pleasant
Charleston W. Va. .	Charleston W. Va. .
Montgomery W. Va.	Montgomery W. Va.
Elkrige W. Va. .	Elkridge
Handale W. Va . . .	Handley
Muchlou, W.Va. .	Mucklow
Wacomah, W. Va. .	Wacomah, W. Va. .
Standard, W. Va. .	Standard, W. Va. .
Carbondale, W. Va . . .	Carbondale, W. Va . . .
Canaletton, W. Va. .	Cannelton
Pittsburg Pa..	Pittsburgh Pa
Chicaco ilin;	Chicago Il
Pait. Crik W. Va. .	Paint Creek

He is a native of Vienna and these two gentlemen
are natives of Naples. Those Romans are Protestants.
The republicans were then enemies of the socialists,
but this republican is now always seen together
with a socialist.

My father, mother and sister have come.

This boi your mother and the woman and old
man are ill; I have seen your mother and brothers
I speak to your uncle about my father and
for my sisters; These books are more than mine
my own child was killed.

My translation is better than my sister's
than that of my sister. There are several
gentlemen There is your brother. Here are your
brother. That, (or This,) is the question he put
to me Those (or These) are the questions he put
to me.

16
88
4
13 13

Practicing Writing in Printed English[1]

He is a native of Vienna and these two gentlemen

are natives of Naples. Those Romans are protestants.

The republicans were then in enemies of thi socialistisi

But this republican in now always seen together

with a socialists.

Ma father, mother and sisters have come.

This coi your mother and woman and old

man are ill; I have seen your mother and brothers

I speak to your uncle about my father and

for ma sisters:

Thes books are mine

my own child was killed.

My translation is better than my sister's. than that of ma sister. There are several gentlemen There is your brother. Here are your

brother. That o This is this question he put

to mi. Those or these are the questions he put

to me.

Author Commentary

1. Fedele wrote all the following in printed English. This is a collection of disjointed sentences and random thoughts. Clearly, he is practicing his English grammar and spelling.

Soding il 25/12 1917

Lista dei pacchi ricevuti in Austria

Croce Rossa ricevuti 8

Di casa ricevuti il primo giorno 20/12 1916

Pacchi ricevuti di Casa Totale 18.15 16

giorno 20/ Dicebre ricevuto 3 pacchi con scarpe
pantaloni e maglie e mutande,

Pacchi ricevuti nel 1918 di Ca 1,1,1,1,1

Croce Rosa, 1,1,1

spedisco la fotografia di Borghese il 26 Maggio 1918
in sieme con Di Martino,

List of Packages from Home and the Red Cross

Goding 25/12/1917

Goding 25 December 1917

List dei pacchi ricevuti in Austria

List of the parcels received in Austria

Croce Rossa Ricevuti 8

Red Cross received 8

Do cals ricevuti il pimo giorno 20/12 1916[1]

From home received 20/12/1916

Pacchi ricevuti di casa totale 13 15 16

Parcels from home total of 16

Giorno 20/ Dicebre ricevuto 3 pacchi con scarpe, pantaloni, e maglie e mutanda

The day 20 December I received 3 par—cels with shoes, pants, sweaters, and underwear.

Pacchi riecevuti nel 1918 di casa 1,1,7,7,7,1

Parcels received in 1918 from home 1,1,7,7,7,1

Croce Rosa 7,1,1

Red Cross 7,1,1

Spedisco la fotografia di Borghese, il 26 Magio 1918 insieme con Di Martino[2]

I send the photograph of Borghese, the twenty—sixth of May 1918 together with Di Martino.

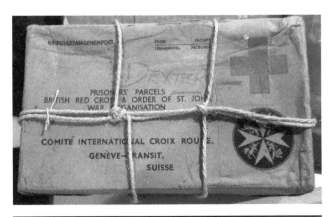

Figure 53: Red Cross parcel

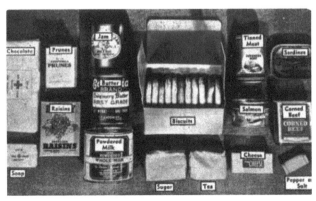

Figure 54: Contents of typical Red Cross parcel

nomi in inglese   James   Giacomo

John   Giovanni

Margaret   Margherita

Henry   Enrico

Frances   Francesca

Jane   Giovanna

Benjamin   Bendamino

Charles 1°   King of England

Bill   Biagio

Jim   Vincenzo

Toni   Antonio

bed, letto church Chiesa market mercato

prison prigione school, scuola table tavola

moon, luna hope, speranza hour, ora,

wool, lana gold oro, lead. piombo earth, terra

wood legno silk seta flax lino, hemp canapa

a gold bracelet, braccialetto, uno braccialetto d'oro,

silk thread, filo di seta, John Creek, lettere

to the king,

Practicing English Names

Fedele is Practicing English Names

Nomi in inglesi (Names in English)

Bed letto church chiesa mar'keti (markets?) mercato market

pris'on prigione prisoner school, scuola table tavola

moon luna hope, speranza hour, ora

?? wool wool lana gold oro, lead. piombo, earth, terra

wood legno silk seta flax lino hemp compra (buy)

a gold bracelet, ???, uno braccialetto doro.

Silk thread filo di seta. John Creek, lattere

To thi King / To the King

Fedele's diary ends here.

Conclusion of the Diary

FEDELE POURED HIS heart out onto the pages of his book. The very private and personal nature of these thoughts would likely not be shared with his fellow prisoners. The diary is one hundred and six years old. In all those years, it is possible that it has never been read by anyone except himself. It had been in his mother's closet for seventy years. It came to light very briefly when Anna Raimondi inherited it. She kept it in her closet for another thirty-six years. The manner and style of his writing is so laborious to read or understand that few would make an effort to read more than a few pages. I consider it a privilege to be the one to undertake this endeavor. His diary is more than a historical document or an accounting of the times. It is a treasured family heirloom that deserves to be preserved, shared, and passed down through the generations. Through this book, those in his lineage will know him as more than a name on the family tree. They will know him through his thoughts, his words, and the legacy that he left to them.

Figure 55: Map of Italy, Austria, and Slovenia

PART II

Documentation

Military Documents and Medals

Figure 56: Commendation for returning to Italy to enlist in the Italian Army

Figure 57: Honorable Discharge Certificate

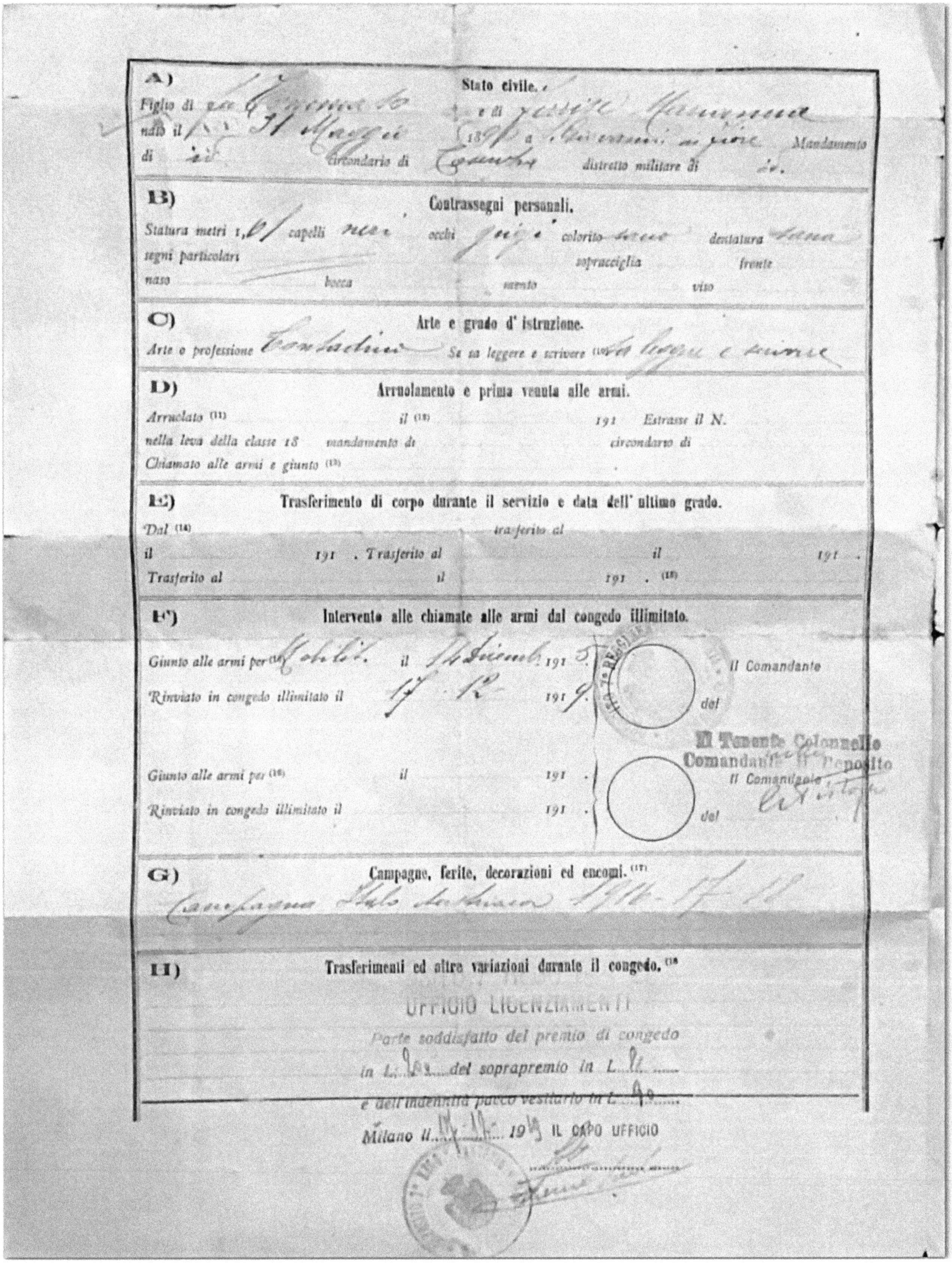

Figure 58: Discharge with good conduct

Figure 59: Gold Commemorative Medal Anniversario Della Vittoria.

THE WWI GOLD Commemorative Medal (or Medaglia—ricordo in ora della 1 Guerra Mondiale in Italia) was an award given to veterans on the 50th anniversary of the victory. The ribbon is designed for display as opposed to being worn on a uniform. It consists of twelve stripes of green-white-red. The same colors and sequence as seen in the Italian flag.

The medal was struck from 24-karat gold with a mirror finish. Each medal weighs 5 grams, or about 1/6 of an ounce. The obverse side bears a small star and an "Adrian" helmet over a laurel and oak wreath. The symbol of an oak and laurel wreath dates to the first Olympic games in Greece. The oak and laurel leaf wreaths were presented to the winners. In modern times the oak and laurel wreath has come to represent courage in battle, victory, and subsequent peace. The

Lamerato sisters provided these photos of the 50th anniversary medal.

To say that Fedele earned this medal is a vast understatement. He gave up four years of his life in service to his country. During that time, he survived brutal combat, months in the alpine trenches, combat wounds, and emergency surgery, followed by life in a concentration camp, where death by beating, starvation, or disease was a constant threat.

Fedele received this medal a few years before he passed away. I believe that he would have a deep appreciation for this medal that we could not understand. It is likely that this medal was one of his prized possessions. His daughters remember that he kept it in a small bowl on the dresser next to his bed. Today its location is unknown. His good friend, Salvatore "Sam" Lamerato, earned the same medal. These are photos of the medal received by Sam Lamerato.

Figure 60: Reverse of Gold Commemorative Medal Anniversario Della Vittoria.

Two of the medals that Fedele would have been eligible for were awarded after he returned to America in 1920. One of those medals was the Commemorative Medal for the Italo-Austrian War 1915–1918 for returning to Italy. The other was the Medal for the War Volunteer. Every one of the brothers would have been qualified to receive these medals. We do not know if Fedele applied for or received either of these medals. Even if he did not receive them, he earned them with his blood, sweat, tears, and four years of his life.

Figure 61: Louis Ferris and Fedele Loria, 1948

Personal Documents

ESTRATTO PER RIASSUNTO DAL REGISTRO
DEGLI ATTI DI NASCITA

ANNO 1896 PARTE SERIE N. 285

L'UFFICIALE DELLO STATO CIVILE

Visti i registri degli atti di nascita di questo Comune

Certifica che LORIA FEDELE
di sesso MASCHILE
è nato in SAN GIOVANNI IN FIORE alle ore VENTI e minuti ZERO
del giorno TRENTA del mese di MAGGIO dell'anno 1896
nella casa posta in Via Coschino
Paternità: LORIA TOMMASO
Maternità: FERRISE MARIANNA

ANNOTAZIONI

NESSUNA.

(Ai sensi dell'art. 3 D.P.R. 2/5/1957 n. 432)

Ai sensi dell'articolo 106 del D.P.R. 3 novembre 2000, n. 396, si rilascia **per estratto dall'originale**, in esenzione dall'imposta di bollo, come previsto dall'art. 7 della Legge 29 dicembre 1990, n. 405.

VALIDO ALL'ESTERO

Il presente estratto ha validità sei mesi dalla data odierna (art. 41, comma 1, D.P.R. 28.12.2000, n. 445).

San Giovanni in Fiore, lì 06 LUG. 2016

Il compilatore ....

COMUNE DI SAN GIOVANNI IN FIORE — Timbro

L'Ufficiale dello Stato Civile
L'UFFICIALE DI STATO CIVILE
Alessio Cotronino

Figure 62: Fedele's birth certificate reissued in 2016

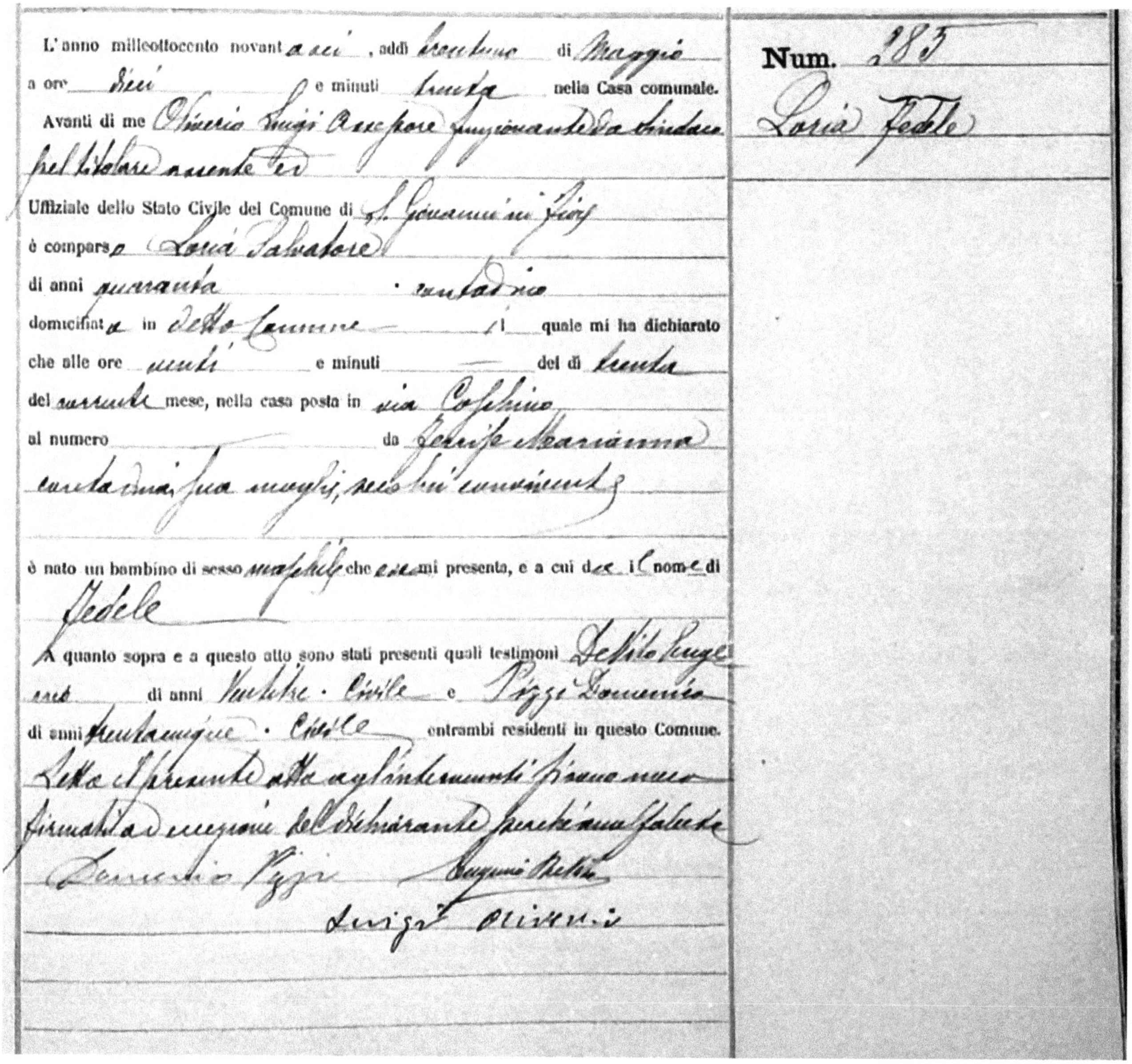

L'anno milleottocento novant*a sei*, addì *trentuno* di *Maggio*

a ore *dieci* e minuti *trenta* nella Casa comunale.

Avanti di me *Olivieri Luigi Anziano funzionante da Sindaco*

pel titolare assente ed

Uffiziale dello Stato Civile del Comune di *S. Giovanni in Fiore*

è comparso *Loria Salvatore*

di anni *quaranta* *contadino*

domiciliat*o* in *detto Comune* il quale mi ha dichiarato

che alle ore *venti* e minuti ——— del dì *trenta*

del *corrente* mese, nella casa posta in *via Coschino*

al numero ——— da *Scrivo Marianna*

casalinga sua moglie, seco lui convivente

è nato un bambino di sesso *maschile* che *essa* mi presenta, e a cui d*à* il nome di

Fedele

A quanto sopra e a questo atto sono stati presenti quali testimoni *Scrivo Luigi*

ecc di anni *ventitre* *Civile* e *Pizzi Domenico*

di anni *trentacinque* *Civile* entrambi residenti in questo Comune.

Letto il presente atto agl'intervenuti si sono meco sotto-
firmati ad eccezione del dichiarante perché analfabeta

Domenico Pizzi *Eugenio Scrivo*

Luigi Olivieri

Loria Fedele

Figure 63: Fedele's original birth certificate from state archives in Cosenza

11/28/21, 9:46 AM   Fedele Loria, "West Virginia Marriages, 1780-1970" • FamilySearch

Spouse's Birth Year
(Estimated)   **1908**

Spouse's Father's Name   **John**

Spouse's Mother's Name   **Annie**

Source Reference   **County Records**

Record Number   **360**

Fedele Loria's Parents and Siblings   OPEN ALL

Tom   Father   M   ⌄

Mary   Mother   F   ⌄

Fedele Loria's Spouses and Children   CLOSE ALL

Katie Pedro   Wife   F 16y   ⌃

Event Type   **marriage**

Name   **Fedele Loria**

Event Type   **Marriage**

Age   **27 years**

Age   **27y**

Age   **27**

Age   **27y**

Birth Year (Estimated)   **1897**

Marriage Date   **01 Mar 1924**

Marriage Date   **1 Mar 1924**

Marriage Place   **Montgomery, Fayette, West Virginia**

Father's Name   **Tom**

Mother's Name   **Mary**

Cite This Record

"West Virginia Marriages, 1780-1970," database, *FamilySearch* (https://familysearch.org/ark:/61903/1:1:FT38-5NH : 11 February 2018), Fedele Loria and Katie Pedro, 01 Mar 1924; citing Montgomery, Fayette, West Virginia, p 101, county clerks, West Virginia; FHL microfilm 494,264.

Copy Citation

Family Tree

ATTACH TO FAMILY TREE

Similar Records

Fedele Loria
West Virginia Marriages, 1780-1970

Figure 64: Record of Fidele's marriage

Fedele became a citizen of the United States of America in Charleston, West Virginia May 18, 1926.

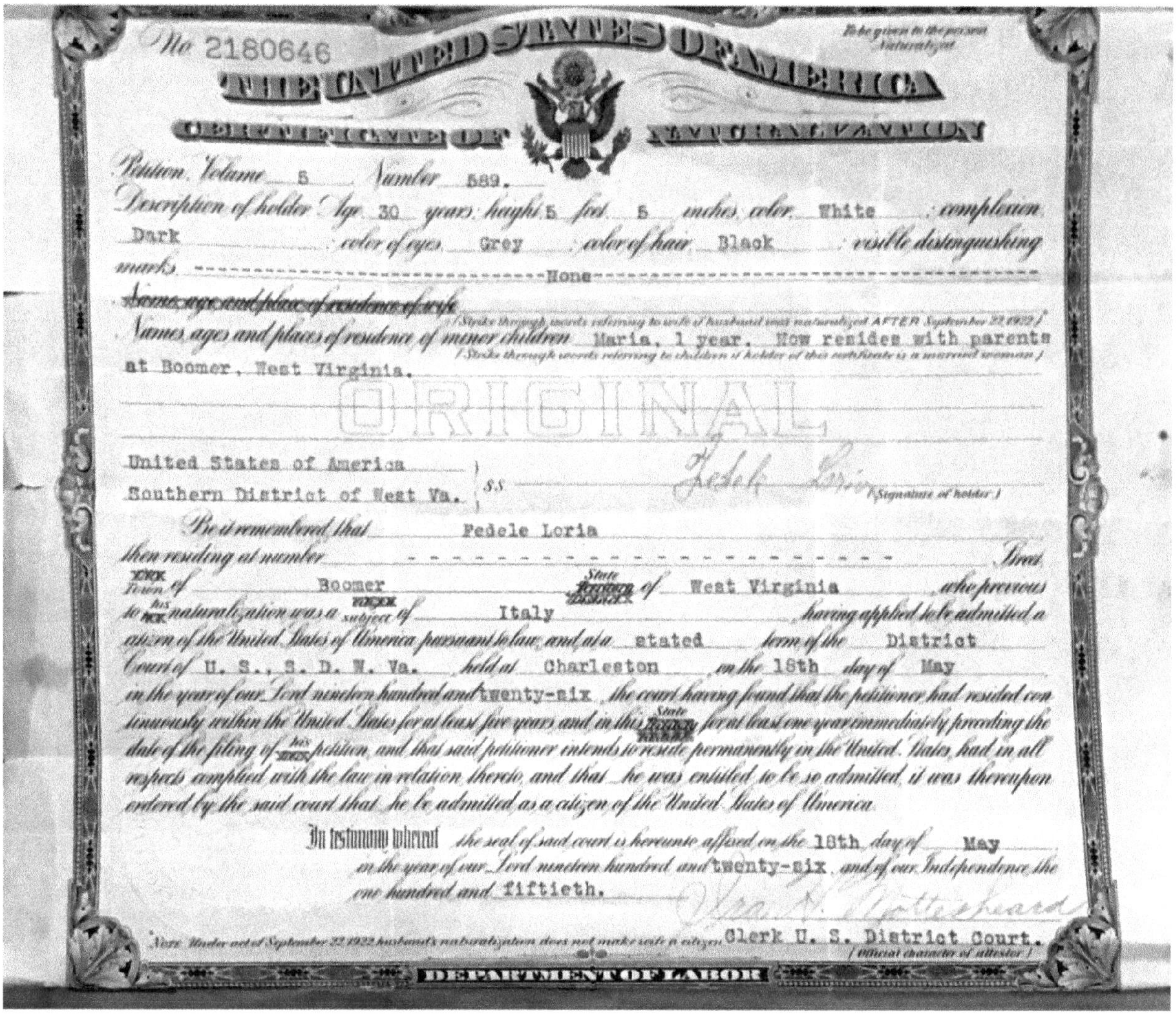

No 2180646

To be given to the person Naturalized

THE UNITED STATES OF AMERICA

CERTIFICATE OF NATURALIZATION

Petition, Volume 5 Number 589.

Description of holder: Age 30 years; height 5 feet 5 inches; color White ; complexion Dark ; color of eyes Grey ; color of hair Black ; visible distinguishing marks ---None---

~~Name, age and place of residence of wife~~

(Strike through words referring to wife if husband was naturalized AFTER September 22, 1922)

Names, ages and places of residence of minor children Maria, 1 year. Now resides with parents at Boomer, West Virginia.

(Strike through words referring to children if holder of this certificate is a married woman)

ORIGINAL

United States of America } SS
Southern District of West Va. }

Fedele Loria (Signature of holder)

Be it remembered that Fedele Loria then residing at number ---- Street, Town of Boomer State of West Virginia who previous to his naturalization was a subject of Italy having applied to be admitted a citizen of the United States of America pursuant to law, and at a stated term of the District Court of U. S., S. D. W. Va. held at Charleston on the 18th day of May in the year of our Lord nineteen hundred and twenty-six the court having found that the petitioner had resided continuously within the United States for at least five years and in this State for at least one year immediately preceding the date of the filing of his petition, and that said petitioner intends to reside permanently in the United States, had in all respects complied with the law in relation thereto, and that he was entitled to be so admitted, it was thereupon ordered by the said court that he be admitted as a citizen of the United States of America.

In testimony whereof the seal of said court is hereunto affixed on the 18th day of May in the year of our Lord nineteen hundred and twenty-six and of our Independence the one hundred and fiftieth.

Clerk U. S. District Court.
(Official character of attestor)

Note: Under act of September 22, 1922 husband's naturalization does not make wife a citizen

DEPARTMENT OF LABOR

Figure 65: Certificate of Naturalization

Passport and Immigration Documents

WHEN FEDELE CAME to America the first time, in 1912, he did not need a passport. Now, after the war, Fedele's friend, Salvatore Benecasa writes to Fedele to notify him of the passport requirements.

> 2/2, 1920 Naples
>
> My best friend I respond to you to let you know that I have come to Naples. You need certification from the mayor but without witness to declare the day you came from America and got off the boat, and it is enough to have your passport is enough to come and you will find me. With many greetings your friend
>
> *Benecasa Salvatore*

Figure 66: Cartolina postale to Signor Loria Fedele

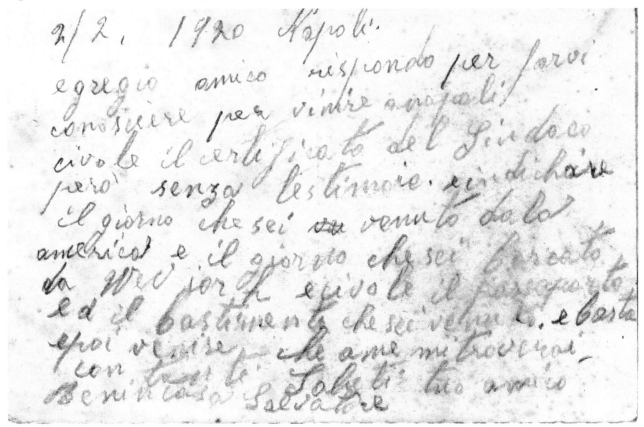

Figure 67: Reverse of Cartolina postale dated 2/2 1920

Page one is *Visa for identity of Signor Loria Fedele, son of Tomasso 14 January 1920.* Page two is details of the owner, such as height 5'2", age 24, eye and hair color chestnut, body type normal.

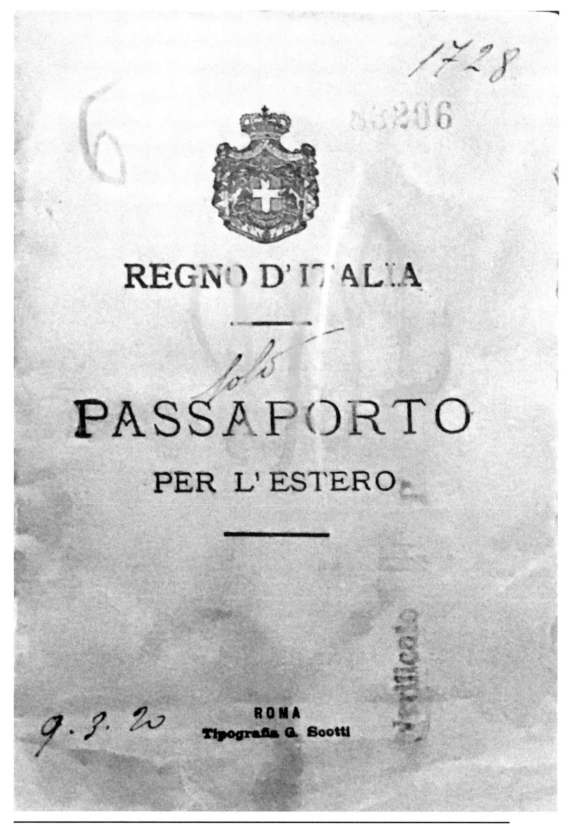

Figure 68: Cover of Fedele's passport

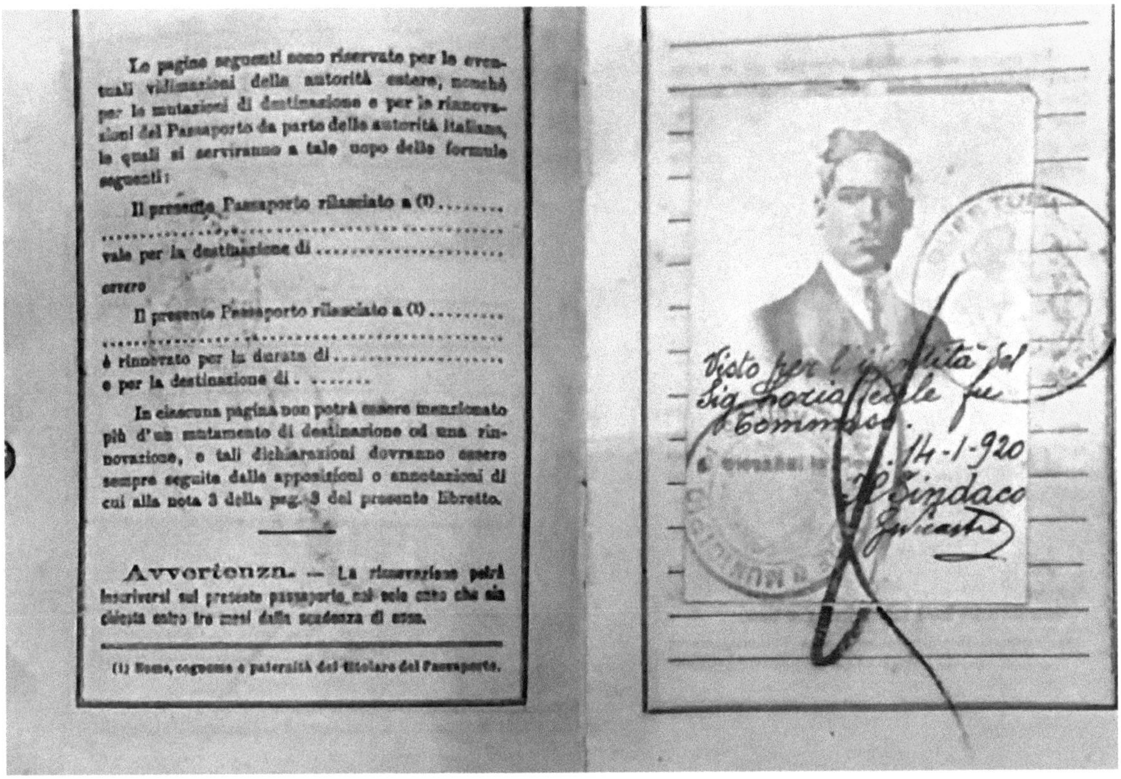
Le pagine seguenti sono riservate per le eventuali vidimazioni delle autorità estere, nonchè per le mutazioni di destinazione e per le rinnovazioni del Passaporto da parte delle autorità italiane, le quali si serviranno a tale uopo delle formule seguenti:

Il presente Passaporto rilasciato a (1) ....
....
vale per la destinazione di ....

ovvero

Il presente Passaporto rilasciato a (1) ....
....
è rinnovato per la durata di ....
e per la destinazione di . ...

In ciascuna pagina non potrà essere menzionato più d'un mutamento di destinazione od una rinnovazione, e tali dichiarazioni dovranno essere sempre seguite dalle apposizioni o annotazioni di cui alla nota 3 della pag. 3 del presente libretto.

Avvertenza. — La rinnovazione potrà inscriversi sul presente passaporto, nel solo caso che sia chiesta entro tre mesi dalla scadenza di esso.

(1) Nome, cognome e paternità del titolare del Passaporto.

Visto per l'identità del Sig. Loria Fedele fu Tommaso
14-1-920
Il Sindaco

Figure 69: Passport pg 1

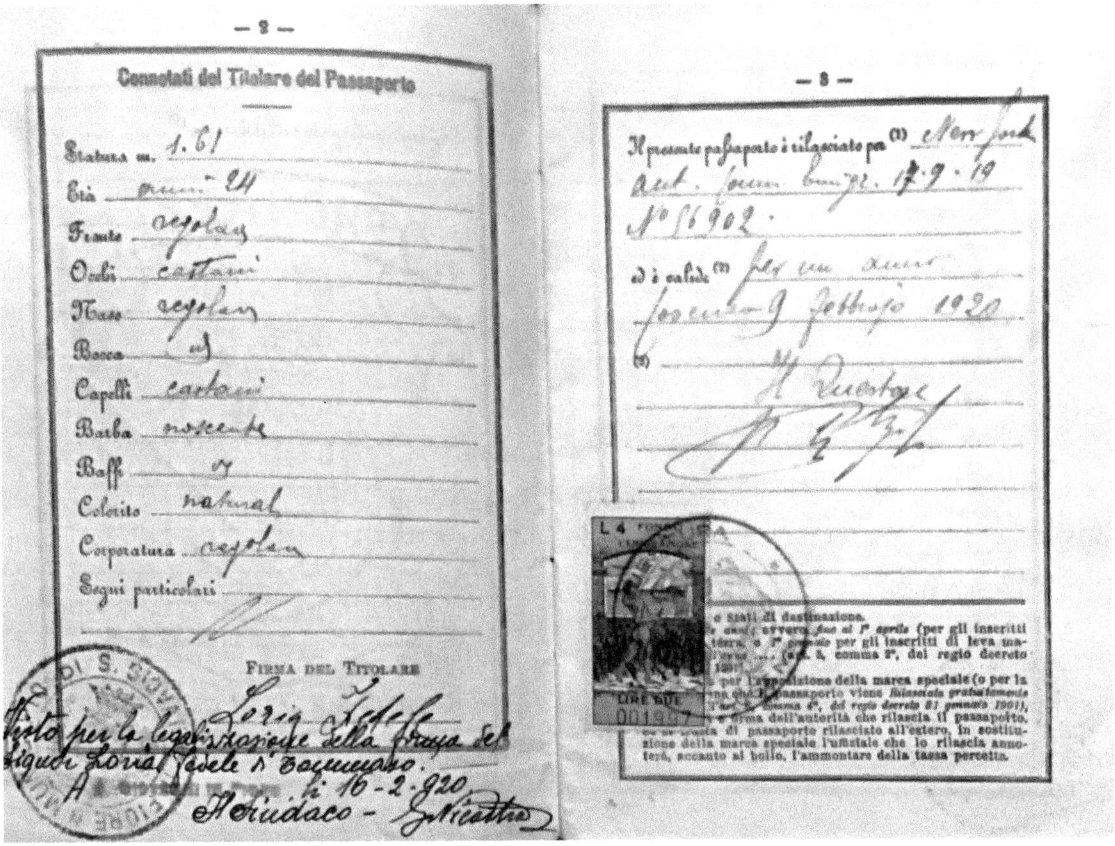
— 2 —

Connotati del Titolare del Passaporto

Statura m. 1.61
Età anni 24
Fronte regolare
Occhi castani
Naso regolare
Bocca id
Capelli castani
Barba nascente
Baffi id
Colorito naturale
Corporatura regolare
Segni particolari

Firma del Titolare
Loria Fedele

Visto per la legalizzazione della firma del Signor Loria Fedele fu Tommaso
li 16-2-920
Il Sindaco

— 3 —

Il presente passaporto è rilasciato per (1) New York
aut. ... 17-9-19
N° 56902

ed è valido (2) per un anno
fino al 9 febbraio 1920

(3)
Il Questore

L 4
LIRE DUE
001997

Figure 70: Passport pgs 2–3

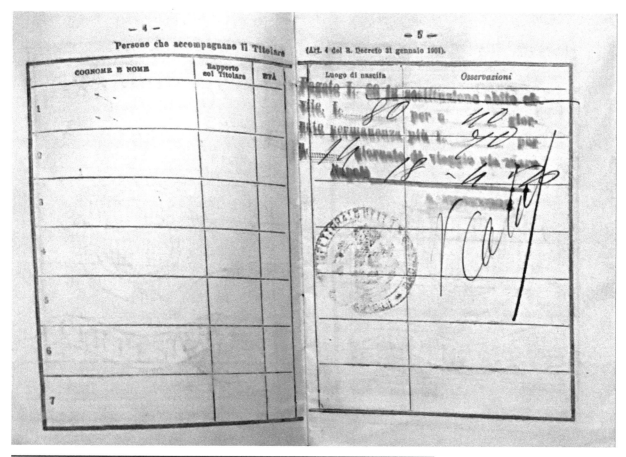

Figure 71: Passport pgs 4–5

Bottom of page two: Two weeks after Fedele received the postcard from his friend in Naples, Fedele's passport was stamped by the mayor of San Giovanni in Fiore. It is dated February 16, 1919. This certifies that he did return to Italy from America. He has met the requirement allowing him to return to America. This is the same date on his commendation for returning to Italy to enlist in the Army. I suspect the mayor's office had the blank standard commendation forms on file. If you look closely, you can see that there is a different spacing and font for the words "Roma 16 Febbraio 1919." The handwriting on the form appears to belong to Fedele. I assume that the mayor's office either took his word that he had been in America, or Fedele was personally known in the office, and they knew he had been in America. I suspect the latter to be more likely.

Page three of the passport is stamped on February 9 and valid for travel to New York any time within one year. Page five shows that he purchased his boat ticket on the eighteenth of April 1920. He paid 80 Lira for the time he stayed in Naples. The price of his boat ticket was 70 Lira.

Fedele and his brother, Giovanni, departed from Naples on April 19, 1920. Their names are on page one of the New York Passenger Arrival to Ellis Island, lines twenty-six and twenty-seven.

Figure 72: Ellis Island passenger list pg 1

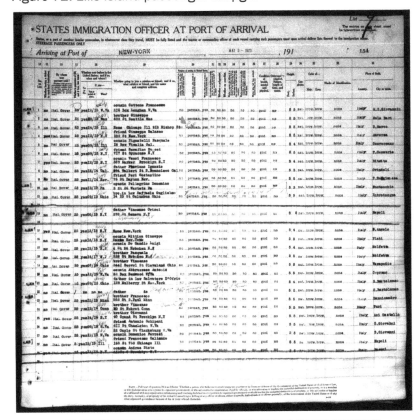

Figure 73: Ellis Island passenger list pg 2

Correspondence Letters and Postcards

FEDELE WAS IN the 135th regiment 5th company in Milan. He sent his mother a postcard, dated 20 September 1919. *Dearest Mother, I had a good vacation. I hope all is well with you and the others, I send greetings to all, my sister-in-law and my sister and brother. I ask for your blessing. With affection son Fedele Loria.* He did not have a vacation; this is an understated sarcastic reference to the nearly four years he has been in trenches and in prison.

Figure 74: Postcard from Fedele to his mother

Figure 75: Reverse of postcard from Fedele to his mother

Figure 76: Buy War Bonds. The lady in white represents Italy, the Huns from the north are the barbarian invaders.

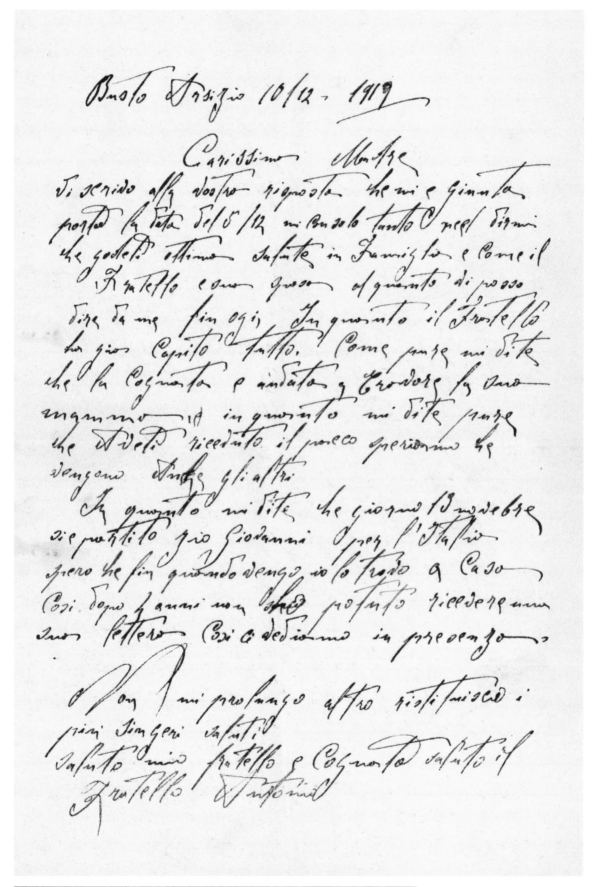

Figure 77: Letter to mother. Coming home soon. pg 1

Busto Arsizio 10/12/1919[1]

Dearest Mother

I am writing your response to your letter that reached me and is dated 5/12. I am very comforted in hearing that you say you are all well in the family and also my brother and his wife. (His brother is Giovanni, married to Costanza. See the timeline of May 3, 1920.) I can say the same of myself up to today. With regard to my brother, I already understood everything. As well you tell me that my sister—in—law has gone to visit her mother. As well you tell me that also that you have received the package, hoping the others arrive also.

You said on the 13 of November Uncle John left for Italy. (His uncle John is the brother to Antonino Ferrise, see the timeline of August 3, 1902, and fall of 1919.) I hope when I come I will find him at home. So, after four years I have not been able to receive his letters. So, we will see each other in person.

I don't want to go on too long with other things. Greetings to my brother (Giovanni) and my sister—in—law (Costanza.) greeting to my brother Antonio.

Author Commentary

1. This is the name of a small town in Northern Italy in the foothills of the Alps.

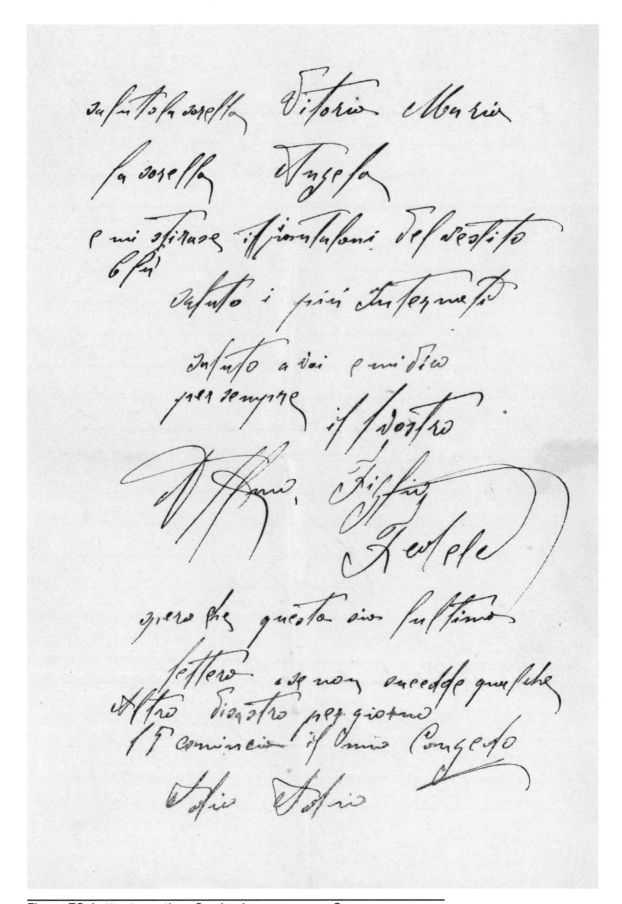

Figure 78: Letter to mother. Coming home soon. pg 2

Greeting sister Vitoria, Maria

The sister, Angela

She ironed my dress pants f my blue suit (for me)

Greeting to all of you (this is a warm and intimate version of greeting—and I (tell you)

Forever always you're your most affectionate son Fedele.

I hope this is the last letter

and if some other disaster does not happen in the next few days,

The fifteenth begins my discharge from the army.

Adio Adio[1]

Author Commentary

1. The words Adio Adio can have multiple meanings. The most common would be simply Goodbye, Goodbye. Another use would be when someone is near death. It could mean, I go to God- or Go to God. I those days and in this context, there is a deeper meaning. If it is God's will, or If It is pleasing to God, then I will see you soon.

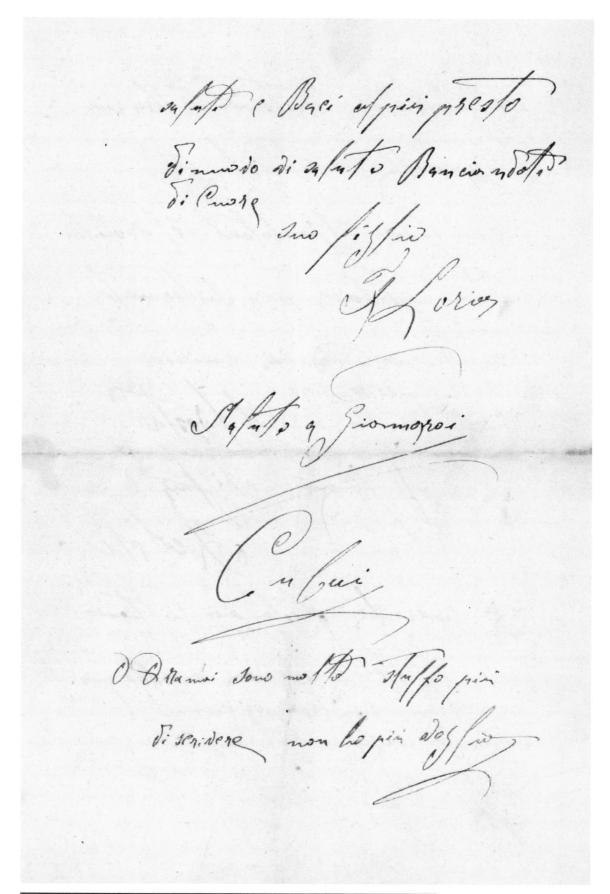

Figure 79: Letter to mother. Coming home soon. pg 3

Greetings and kisses, as soon as possible

greeting, big kisses with all my heart.

Your son

F. Loria

Salute Gio??

Sono molto stuffo pi`u

Vi scrivere non ho pi`u voglio

Greetings to Gio??

At this point I am very tired of writing

I no longer want to write anymore.

AUTHOR'S NOTE

So much is lost in the translation to English. This is a heartfelt letter full of love to all his family. His feeling of passionate love for his family jumps off the pages when read aloud in Italian. Even if you do not read Italian, you can see and feel his emotion by looking at the way he crafted this letter from the heart. This is not the normal way a man would write to his mother. In those days, men were generally not this expressive with their feelings, especially so in writing. This letter and its tone are completely in line with the way he expressed his feelings throughout the diary. No doubt, his mother would have treasured this letter for the good news it brought to her and her home. The last of her three soldier sons would be home soon. A hole in her heart was about to be filled.

In our times, nobody handwrites a letter. We type with spell check, and we can make copies with a single keystroke. E-mail can traverse continents in a second. Discarding a sheet of paper is done without thought. Not so in 1917. Paper, ink, and a quill pen were expensive, almost a luxury. When Fedele wrote this letter, he did so with forethought and care. His letter carries more than words on paper. He knew his mother would read and re-read it many times and then preserve it. He conveys the very essence of what he values most, and those feelings leaped off the page and into his mother's heart, filling that hole.

Figure 80: Postcard from Giovanni Loria

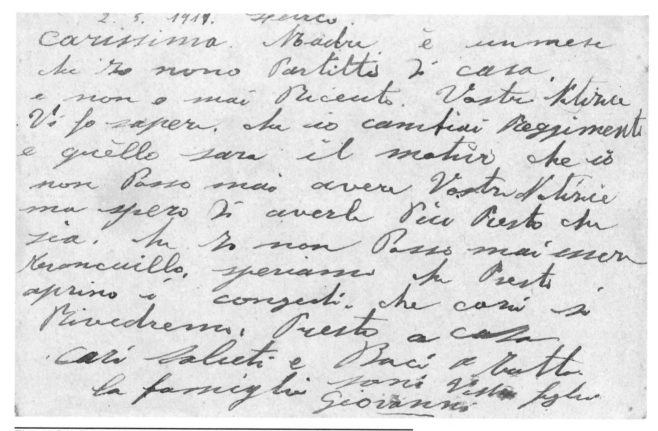

Figure 81: Reverse of postcard from Giovanni Loria

2 May 1919

Dearest mother, it was one month ago that we left home and I never hear from you. I am letting you know that I changed regiments. That could be the reason why I never heard from you. But can you send it as soon as possible. I can never be at rest peace—fully, I hope that my discharge will be soon. So with this you will soon be able to see me at home. Warm greeting and kisses to all the family. I am your son, Giovanni

Figure 82: Postcard two from Giovanni Loria

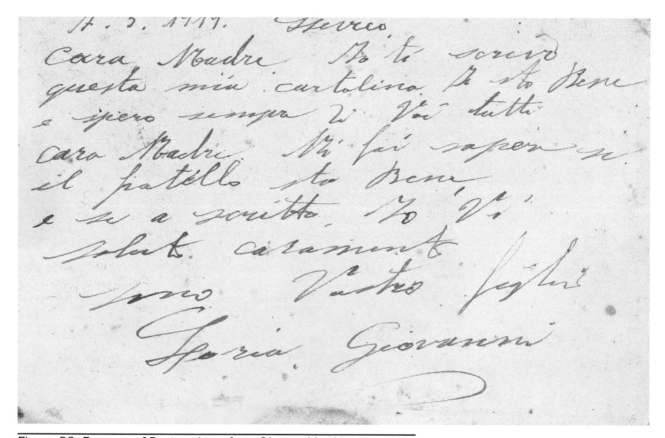

Figure 83: Reverse of Postcard two from Giovanni Loria

17 May 1919

Dear Mother, I write to you this postcard. I am fine and I hope ????? all of you. Dear mother let my brothers know that I am well.[1]

Most loving greetings I am your son

Giovanni Loria[2]

Author Commentary

1. The return address is the 82nd regiment, 5th company, war zone.
2. We know little about the military service of his brothers Giovanni and Antonio. From this letter, we can conclude that they survived the war and that they came home before Fedele. Giovanni wrote two postcards to his mother in April of 1919, five months after the war ended. It is speculation, but it is possible that Giovanni was among the 250,000 former prisoners awaiting inquiry or trial after the war. This could explain why he was delayed in returning home.

Figure 84: Italian Discount Bank (Buy Bonds)

PART III

Considering the Past, Present, and Future

"A person without knowledge of their past history, origin and culture is like a tree without roots." —Marcus Garvey

A Journey of Discovery—Finding Our Roots

IN THE FALL of 2015, I was challenged and inspired by one of our cousins to search for our roots by finding our long-lost living relatives in Italy. She encouraged me when for months, I found nothing and no one. We shared the excitement of finding each new clue to the history of our family and our roots. Without her help and encouragement, this would have been a short journey without discovery. I had no idea how many surprises and discoveries were to come. The biggest surprise, by far, has been the discovery of the diary written by Feldele Loria. For inspiring me to begin this journey of discovery, all of us owe a very special thank you to our cousin, Roselie Ferris Price.

We have another cousin who shares this same passion and love of our heritage. Patti Lorea Shears provided one of the two keys to finding our family and roots in Italy. She went to San Giovanni in Fiore in the summer of 2016 in search of living relatives. With assistance from our dear friend and translator, Antonella Prosperati, they were able to obtain the birth certificate of her grandfather, Fedele Loria, also known as Felix Loria. During her brief time in San Giovanni in Fiore, Patti was not successful in finding our living relatives. She left the birth certificate with Antonella, who promised to continue the search.

The other key was provided by the Lamerato sisters. Gina, Vicky, Angelina, and Rose of Hamtramck, Michigan. They provided me with a small family tree written by their mother, Vittoria Giramonte. Vittoria remembered the names of her aunts and uncles in the Ferrise family from her youth in San Giovanni in Fiore, Calabria, Italy. I sent the tree to Antonella. With these two

Figure 85: Roselie Ferris Price

keys, the birth certificate, and the family tree, she began her search. After six months of persistent effort, she found Anna Raimondi Marazita. Anna recognized the names of her great aunts and uncles who were on the Ferrise family tree. She immediately recognized the name of her uncle, Fedele Loria, on the birth certificate. When Anna was much younger, she had exchanged letters with her uncle Fedele in America. With a stroke of luck, Antonella found Anna, who is descended from both the Loria and Ferrise families. Anna was so very excited at the prospect of renewing contact with her American family. I recall the first video conference call with her soon after finding her. If she could have come through the computer screen to hug me, I believe she would have done so. Anna had inherited this long-forgotten diary. We owe a debt of gratitude to Antonella, Roselie, Patti, and the

Lamerato sisters. They have a deep love of family and our Italian roots. Without their help, we may never have known about our cousins in Italy, or this nearly forgotten heirloom diary.

I believe with all my heart that Fedele lives on with us in spirit. Surely, he would be pleased to know that his great-grandchildren can read his written words. I doubt that he ever imagined such a thing.

In June of 2017, I arrived in San Giovanni in Fiore, along with my wife, Marie, our sons, Joe and Jonny, and my first cousin, Beverly Ferris Davison and her son, Jesse. We were a group of six and made quite the stir in town among our many cousins there. The next morning, we had a family meeting in the conference room of the hotel, La Duchessa della Sila. Perhaps fifteen of our cousins were present. Oh, what an exciting time that was! Everyone was talking all at once, in Italian, of course. As Americans, we understood little, but we could feel the excitement and love in that room. At the time, my Italian language skills were exceptionally weak. Maybe I could understand one person in a quiet room. But in this crowd, I could understand little. Our translator, Antonella, was so patient, and just barely able to maintain order in the room!

I was seated next to Anna Ramondi Marazita. On her lap was a clear plastic bag full of photos, some letters, and **THE DIARY**. I understood little of what she said. However, I did recognize that little book to be important. I asked my wife, Marie, to take a photo of every page. During the whirlwind of activity over the next several days, I completely forgot about the plastic bag and its contents.

Five years later, I happened upon the photos of the diary on my computer. Some of the photos were distorted or out of focus. I was mesmerized by the ancient writing in quill pen. I could make out a few words, like prisoner, Austria, 1917, and the word "hunger," which was repeated several times. So many questions came to mind. How did photos of the diary get into my computer memory? Who was Loria Fedele? Why did he write this book? I stared at the signature for a few minutes. I wondered how this name was pronounced in English. My jaw almost hit the floor when I said the name in English. When I said "Felix Loria" out loud, I had a flashback moment. From my distant memory, I recall the day in 1973 when my mother learned that he had passed away. They were first cousins. I remembered her sadly saying, "He was the last of the ones from San Giovanni." I had never heard of San Giovanni in Fiore prior to that day. Mom had lived near Felix Loria in West Virginia in the 1930s. I remembered my mother talking about this man. That was the moment a seed was planted in me. That conversation/seed was lost and nearly forgotten for sixty years. The moment I said his name in English, I immediately knew this old diary was very important. I knew the book was a historical document. What was a historical document, in my mind, had just become a treasured family heirloom. Fedele has elderly children, grandchildren, and great-great-grandchildren here in America. Most of his descendants did not know he was a prisoner during WWI. I was certain that his diary would be of great interest to them. Now, I was motivated to search for answers to the questions of how these photos got onto my computer and who owned the diary. After looking through hundreds of photos from the 2017 trip, I found my answer. There was a photo of Anna and I together at La Duchessa Della Sila Hotel, and she had the diary in her lap. That is when I knew I was going to write a book.

Now that I recognized the importance of the diary, we arranged a video conference with Anna and her children, Maria, Salvatore, and Giovanni. She explained that Fedele wrote the book while he was a prisoner of war in Austria during the winter of 1917. When he left Italy in 1920 to return to

America, he left the book with his mother, Marianna Ferrise. For more than seventy-five years, the book was forgotten in a closet. Anna inherited the house from her grandmother, Marianna. While cleaning the house, one of Anna's sons found the diary. She has kept it safe for the last thirty-five years. During my video conference with the family, I asked them to mail me a photocopy of each page. Because my Italian language skills were weak, they misunderstood me. A couple of weeks later, I received not photocopies, but the most precious original. I promised to return it to her. I hope to fulfill that promise by personally delivering the original diary and a copy of this book to Anna in the summer of 2023.

For hundreds of years, the Loria and Ferrise families have lived in San Giovanni. How many generations have lived in the neighborhood called "Via Vallone"? The families of Via Vallone were members of the parish church, Santa Maria Della Grazia—Saint Mary of Grace. Our family church, also known as The Mother Church, is almost 400 years old. It was established in 1527 and is located about thirty yards from the Loria and Ferrise family homes. How many of our ancestors have been baptized, married, and had their funerals at this altar? We don't know the answers to those ques-

Figure 86: Santa Maria Della Grazie/Saint Mary of Grace Church

tions, but we do know these two things. The first is that the Loria and Ferrise lines live on in each of us. The second is that our roots run deep in this neighborhood.

Roots in Italy—Dreams in America

WHEN FEDELE WAS mining coal, I wonder, what were his goals? Did he have dreams for the future for himself and his family? What were his expectations for the next month, next year, the next generation, and after that? I suspect that his immediate goal would be to put food on the table and keep a roof over his family. Fedele was better educated than most at that time. He knew that a high school diploma would mean not having to work in the mines. No doubt, he had an expectation that each of his children would finish high school. From the bottom of a coal mine, it would be hard to see far beyond those modest goals. Could he have hoped that one day some of his grandchildren would graduate from college? Maybe, but that would have been a sky-high dream for a coal miner. Anything that he could have dreamed of for his descendants in the next few generations has been far surpassed. Every one of his eight children graduated from high school. Among his descendants, there are at least eight advanced college degrees. A partial list of the occupations among his descendants includes a personal injury attorney, a registered nurse, a crane operator, three teachers, a legislative assistant to Vice President Biden, a dental hygienist, and a captain in the US Army.

Fedele's son, Sam, had four daughters. Sam was not able to follow the Italian tradition of giving the first son the name of his grandfather. One of Sam's daughters, Patti, gave her first child the unusual first name of Lorea to honor the memory of her beloved grandfather. Lorea Stallard has made us all proud. The woman that carries Fedele's name has worked with officials at the highest levels of our government. Here is an excerpt from one of her facebook posts.

"I'm just a girl from West Virginia—the great-granddaughter of a coal miner and immigrants. If you told me five years ago that I would be in the same room as the Pope, watch John Lewis triumphantly walk across the Edmund Pettus bridge in Selma, and shake hands with the President of the United States, I never would have believed you."

Figure 87: Lorea Stallard, legislative assistant to Vice President Air Force 2

Figure 88: Map of Italy

His Roots, His Reasons

MANY OF OUR ancestors had difficult and often short lives. They were bound to San Giovanni in Fiore by poverty, tradition, and illiteracy. Fortunately, Fedele learned to write. He was able to express himself clearly. In his writing, we can see hope, his devotion to his mother, wit, sarcasm, and at times, deep despair. He wrote this diary during the worst days of his life. Through his writing, he conveys those three things that sustained and motivated him. They are his faith in God, hope for a better future, and above all, the love of his family.

He learned early on to place his faith in the Catholic church and all its traditions. His faith sustained him through poverty, brutal combat, hunger in the prison camp, and more than thirty-five years in the mines. He would have learned those beliefs from the example of his father, Salvatore/Tommaso Loria, and his mother, Marianna Ferrise. He, in turn, taught his set of beliefs and family values by example to his eight children. "Poppy," as he was known by his family, never missed Sunday mass at St. Antony's Shrine in Boomer, West Virginia. Fedele was known to have said many prayers in the name of St. Anthony. His surviving daughters, Malfalda, Genevieve, Marguerite, and Mary, told me that their Poppy taught them these values early in life. That influence persists in his daughter, Mary, who, at age ninety-eight, still has some prayer time every day.

Coal miners are, by definition, poor. While it is true that they never had a lot, they had enough. Fedele and his wife, Katie, had a home full of love and old-world values. Poppy brought with him the only gold to be found in Calabria. That is the heart of gold that good parents pass on through generations. Everyone who carried his name did so with good manners and the right amount of family pride. Malfalda said, "Poppy always paid his bills, always on time." He understood the value of a good name. The police never came to his door. In those days of the early 1900s, prejudice against poor immigrants was a common occurrence. The discrimination was not severe, but it was there. In the 1920s, new legislation severely limited the number of immigrants coming to America. Many immigrants, especially those from southern Italy, were widely considered to be inherently inferior, even a different race. As such, they were often treated as second-class citizens.

The new laws allowed the immigrants more of an equal opportunity. Their children were more integrated into their communities. They may have spoken Italian in the home, but they spoke English without an accent at school. Opportunities denied their parents were open to them. Fedele's children were able to climb the socioeconomic ladder. They Americanized their last name to assimilate into American society more smoothly. The Loria name was changed to Lorea because that is how an English speaker would phonetically spell the name. Italian immigrants were sometimes referred to as "Tallys." While this is a pejorative term, the Lorea/Loria family and other Italians referred to each other as Tallys, and they did so with pride. Their small mining town of Boomer had the second-largest population of Italian immigrants in WV. This was a tight-knit community. They were proud of their heritage. Malfalda and his grandson, Bobby Lorea, agreed on one philosophy they learned from Poppy, "We take care of each other." Malfalda recalls that Poppy and Mommy would write to the family back in Italy. Most letters would include some hard-earned cash. Our cousin Anna Raimondi Marazita remembers writing and receiving some of those letters. She would read them to her grandmother, Marianna Ferrise, and her aunts and uncles, who were Fedele's siblings.

His love of family shines through when writing about his mother and their home. We see it in his diary entry dated December 24, 1917. He feels her aching heart because her son was being held prisoner on Christmas eve. He imagines his mother sick with worry. She had good reason to worry. All three of her sons were in combat zones. He feels her pain as she absent-mindedly prepares her home for Christmas while he suffers. Clearly, he loved his mother and their home. In his mind, he hears the melodic ringing of the church bells on Christmas morning. Memories of children in their innocence singing praises to the baby Jesus come to him, then his daydream is shattered by the harsh reality that surrounded him. On that Christmas eve, Fedele and his fellow prisoners lived one of the darkest days of their lives. He writes of quiet sobbing and overwhelming melancholy. It seems they will never see their homes or families again. Many years later, after he became a family man, how could he not relive the memories of his own childhood as he tucked his children in on Christmas Eve? Above all, Fedele was a family man. Some memories are better when preserved. Others, like Christmas Eve 1917, and his diary, are better kept in a forgotten and rarely visited closet.

Fedele was a respected member of the community, in part because he could read and write. Some of the other miners would ask him to read letters from their families in Italy. Then he would write a letter for them in response. Fedele became a US Citizen in 1926. This was one of the proudest days of his life. He had the certificate of Naturalization framed, and it has been hanging on the wall of his living room for the last ninety-seven years. Poppy had become a proud American of Italian descent. He was a proud citizen, but he never forgot where he came from. Through his example, he taught his children the value of Italian culture, their roots, and history.

Every immigrant had to make sacrifices that we could not imagine. To come to America meant saying goodbye to siblings and grieving parents, perhaps forever. They had to leave their home and friends. Behind them in Calabria was grinding poverty. Ahead was an uncertain future. Fedele was only fifteen years on the day he left home. He was the third and youngest son to immigrate to America. This was the third time his parents suffered the grief of separation. Now, three parts of their lives were gone. The pain must have seemed unbearable for them. It would have been a sad day in the Loria home, almost as if they had lost a son. Many sons and husbands went to America to do dangerous jobs, and some never returned.

Fedele's hope for a better future was in America. He joined hundreds of thousands of Italian immigrants who came to America hoping for a better future outside the boundaries of tradition, poverty, and illiteracy. He set off for America with empty pockets and a heart full of hope, and likely, a good dose of trepidation.

He had to find his way to Naples, hopefully by train. The poorest rode a mule or walked the 160 miles. From there, he would take a boat to America. We don't know how he paid for his train or boat tickets. The cost would have been more than most peasant families could afford. The records at Ellis Island do not show any other relatives on the boat with him. There were others on the boat from San Giovanni in Fiore. We can only assume that his parents entrusted a close family friend to care for him. After he arrived at Ellis Island, he would have taken a couple of trains to the coal fields of central/southern West Virginia in the Kanawha River valley.

It is possible that he met one of the labor recruiters that the coal companies sent to San Giovanni. The coal company would pay for the boat and trains, with the agreement to pay back the company through payroll deductions. The company usually had a store that would sell all things a miner would need. Clothing, equipment, groceries, and more. Many miners found themselves hopelessly in debt to the company store. The miners had no protection against the predatory behavior of the coal companies. This was a type of peonage; it was just short of slavery. Eventually, labor laws were enacted, and the miners were able to get out of the bondage of the company store. It is likely that Fedele started coal mining in debt. According to his daughters, Mafalda and Margarete, he always paid his debts. He was able to avoid a lifetime of debt.

We don't know for certain where he lived in the first few years. It is safe to assume that he lived near his uncles, Antonio, Giovanni, and Salvatore, along with his brothers, Giovanni and Antonio. We do know that he lived in Logan during the mid to late 1920s near his friend Sam Lamerato, who was married to Fedele's first cousin Vittoria Giramonte. Some years later, Fedele moved to Boomer, West Virginia, where he married Katie Pedro/Patrella, also known as Anna Marie, and raised his family.

Figure 89: Group photo The Loria/Lorea Family circa 1952. Back row left to right: Angelina, Mary, Genevieve, Sammy Front row left to right: Marguerite, Fedele Felix Loria, Frank, Anna Marie Ninna, Mafaa Jonny is absent because he was in the Air Force, stationed in Korea.

Figure 90: Fedele's mother
Marianna Ferrise Loria (seated)
with daughter, Maria, and son,
Antonio, circa 1925.

Figure 91: Vittoria Loria

Figure 92: Left to right: Giovanni Loria, Anthony Ferris of Boomer,
and Francesco Mancuso

Figure 93: Giovanni Loria and his wife Costanza

These are a few of the photos taken when Anthony was on military leave from Germany in 1953. He gave me copies of those fifty-four-year-old photos. When my family made our first visit to San Giovanni in 2017, we carried many copies of those photos with us. Hearts were touched, and some tears were shed when our cousins saw photos of their grandparents and other long-deceased relatives. For some, it was the first time they had seen a photo of their grandparents in their youth. It warmed my heart to give these photo treasures to our new-found family in San Giovanni. Indelible memories were made that day.

Costanza is wearing the customary dress worn by married women. A woman wearing this traditional dress was respectfully referred to as a pacchiana. The custom of the pacchiana dress faded out in the 1960s. The memory of the pacchiana has a warm spot in the heart of those who remember the traditional dress of their mother or grandmother. Vittoria's dress is the customary attire of an unmarried woman.

The photos were almost certainly taken at the home of Salvatore Mancuso. In one of the photos, Anthony and Salvatore are seated at Salvatore's dining room table. Salvatore's granddaughter, Rosa Pia, showed us that same table. During our visit, I looked for the old stone wall, but it was not there. There is a stone wall in place there now. It is newer and safer than those stacked-up boulders. I am 99 percent sure these photos were taken just outside of Salvatore's carpenter shop at Via Fiume Lese #24. During WWII, the Germans occupied San Giovanni. They looted the carpenter shop and took so many tools that Salvatore was unable to earn a living. For a few years, when Salvatore was a coal miner, he bonded with his family in WV. Those bonds were lasting, and strong enough to reach across an ocean.

Figure 94: Fedele with Jim Schipper and friends

We do not know with certainty the circumstances of this photo or the names of the two friends on the left. Fedele is on the right, with Jim Schipper next to him. He appears to be in his early 20s. I suspect that this photo was made in Boomer, West Virginia, circa 1920–1922.

Boomer, WVa. was the home of Fedele "Felix" Lorea, his wife, Katie, and his children from the mid-1920s to date. Louis Ferris and his family lived only a few blocks away from the 1930s till the early 1960s.

Figure 95: Fedele and Katie on the front porch in Boomer circa 1940

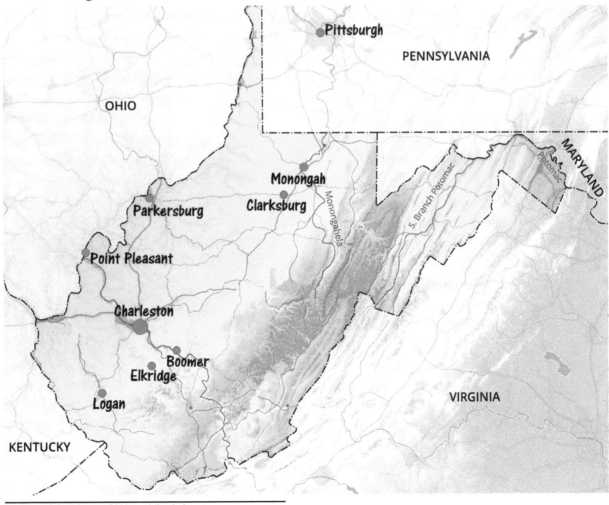

Figure 96: Map of West Virginia

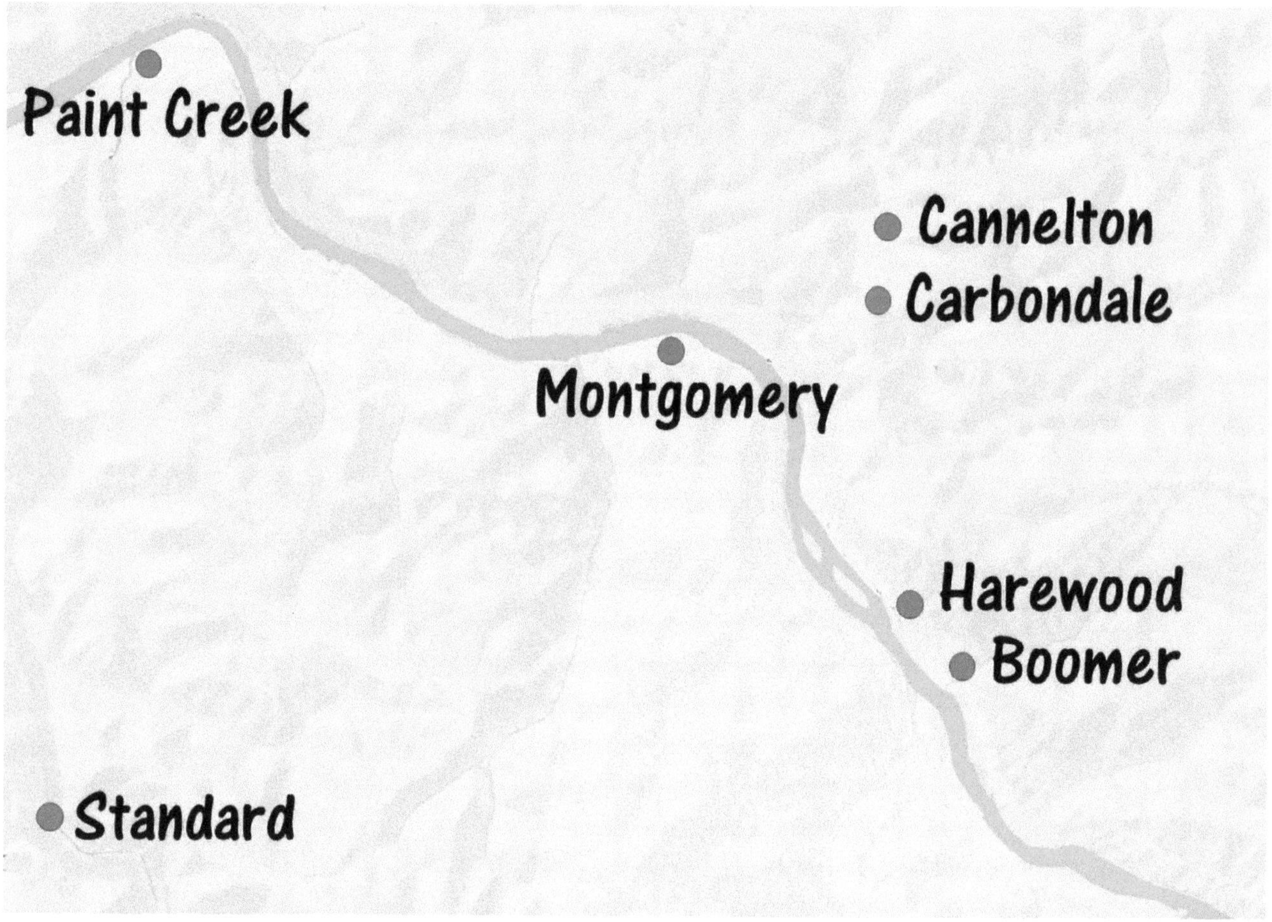

Paint Creek

Cannelton
Carbondale

Montgomery

Harewood
Boomer

Standard

Figure 97: Map of Boomer and surrounding towns

© Pasquale Carbone.

Figure 98: The Emotional Pain of Emigration; Commune di San Giovanni in Fiore, Monongha

Pasquale Carbone, a noted artist in San Giovanni in Fiore, was commissioned to create this mural in 2007. The name of this mural is *Per non Dimenticare*. The translation is "So as not to forget" This one image depicts two causes of the greatest heartache in San Giovanni. The emotional pain of emigration penetrated deeply into the life of this little town. The young man's suffering represents the people who so deeply feel the pangs of emigration. In the background is the Abby, the civic and religious center of his hometown. His roots are firmly planted in his family, the church, and the soil of his homeland. The suitcase represents those who have left, or perhaps he is next to leave. Nearly

Figure 99: The Abby Commune di San Giovanni in Fiore, established in 1202, as it appears today

every family lost someone to emigration. Sometimes entire families would leave. Calabria has always been beautiful, but some believe it was cursed by God. For many, the only choices were to stay and starve or uproot themselves and go to America. The holes where roots have been forcefully pulled represent those who will never return. There are deep emotional scars left on the land. San Giovanni never recovered fully from the mass migration to America. Officials at the national level encouraged emigration. Their reasoning was simply that there would be fewer mouths to feed. The result was that the population in Southern Italy, especially in Calabria, declined dramatically. After-effects of that population drain still linger more than 100 years later. San Giovanni has housing for at least 60,000 people but a population of only 20,000.

The other reason for the mural is to commemorate what is believed to be the worst day in the history of San Giovanni in Fiore. Hundreds of men from San Giovanni went to America to be coal miners. In 1907, many of them died instantly in a coal mine explosion. The enormity of this event and its effect on San Giovanni cannot be overstated. The young man in the painting is displaying the grief felt in all of Calabria. The holes in the ground represent those husbands, fathers, and sons that were lost. The hand of fate is shown as it is about to rip another piece of Calabria out of the ground, never to return.

Figure 100: The Abby, Commune di San Giovanni in Fiore as Fedele would have remembered it in the early 1900s.

Figure 101: Open-air morgue

The Mining Disaster at Monongah

THIS TRAGIC EVENT occurred at Monongah, West Virginia, on December 6, 1907, and has been described as "the worst mining disaster in American history." The explosion occurred in Fairmont Coal Company's No. 6 and No. 8 mines and was one of the contributing events leading to the creation of the United States Bureau of Mines.

According to the official count, 420 men perished. Some said up to 600 died. The exact count will never be known because those on the payrolls often took their children with them into the mines as helpers. An explosion of this magnitude would have killed many of them instantly. The shock wave created incredibly high pressures. The flames instantly consumed all the oxygen, leaving only carbon dioxide to breathe. The roof supports gave way, causing parts of the roof to collapse. Some of the air shafts remained open, but the equipment and fans that delivered fresh air were destroyed. The exact cause of the explosion has not been officially determined. Explosive coal dust was one possibility; another was highly flammable methane gas. The probable source of ignition was either a spark from an electrical wire or the flame from a miner's lamp. There were only five survivors, and they died later from their injuries.

The dead were initially taken to the local morgue. When the morgue became full, the lobby of the First National Bank of Monongah was converted to a temporary morgue. There were so many caskets that within two days, the streets of Monongah became an open-air morgue.

The brothers, Antonio and Giovanni Ferrise, their brother-in-law, Salvatore Mancuso, and their nephews, Antonio and Giovanni Loria, were miners not far from Monongah. Among the dead were 172 Italians, 34 of them were from San Giovanni in Fiore. We cannot know for sure, but it is nearly certain that they personally knew some of the victims. If they did not know the men personally, they would have known their families. This event would have had an enormous impact on every miner. The next day the Ferrises, the Lorias, and thousands of other Italian miners did what they knew they had to do. They got out of bed, put on their headlamp, and went back down into the mines to do one of the most dangerous jobs in the world. There was no other choice if they wanted to feed their families.

The news of this event would have traveled quickly to San Giovanni. Certainly, every family in the town would have been desperate for news of the fate of their loved ones. Most miners moved often and wrote home infrequently, so the family back home could not know if their loved one was in the explosion. Many of the people of San Giovanni could not read or write. The newspaper published a list of victims that would have been read aloud. Wives and mothers would have gathered. Emotions would have been barely under control, while feeling both extreme anxiety and hope. Some did **not** hear the name of their loved one. How would they feel as they heard the shocked cries of anguish from friends and neighbors? I cannot imagine the agony of seeing or hearing the name of your husband or son on that list. Here is a partial list of those who never returned.

Abbruzzino Francesco	Gallo Salvatore	Oliverio Giovanni
Basile Antonio	Girimonte Raffaele	Perri Tommaso
Basile Giovanni	Guarascio Francesco	Pignanelli Saverio
Basile Saverio	Iaconis Giovanni	Provenzale Pietro
Belcastro Giuseppe	Iaconis Francesco	Scalise Luigi
Belcastro Serafino	Lavigna Pasquale	Silletta Antonio
Bitonti Antonio	Leonetti Giovambattista	Urso Gennaro
Bitonti Rosario	Lopez Salvatore	Veglia Antonio
Bonasso Giovanni	Marra Salvatore	Veltri Leonardo
Ferrari Giuseppe		

Year	Number of coal mining fatalities
1907	3,200
1908	2,445
1909	2,642
1910	2,821
1911	2,656
1912	2,419
1913	2,785
1914	2,454
1915	2,269

Five years later, in 1912, Fedele was a fifteen-year-old boy. His mother and father kissed their youngest son goodbye and sent him off to be a coal miner. The memory of the Monongah disaster would have still been fresh in their memory. How hard must life be for the family to do such a thing? They lived in crushing poverty. How desperate would his parents have to be that they would be willing to take a chance with the lives of all three of their sons? It is hard to imagine the depth of grief and

Figure 102: Roger Hill and Antonella Prosperati in 2019, Monument to Miners.

worry his parents felt as their youngest son departed San Giovanni. This was an immense sacrifice by his parents so that their sons might have a better life. It was their hope that despite the risks, Fedele and his brothers would have a chance at the American dream. They sent their child alone across the ocean to do a brutal and dangerous job. Even if he survived the mines, they knew full well that he might never return.

December 7, 1907, may have been the worst day in the history of San Giovanni in Fiore. So that the lost husbands and sons will never be forgotten, a monument to their memory stands at Piazza Aldo Moro. The memorial reads: "Lest we forget the Calabrian miners dead in West Virginia (USA). The sacrifice of those strong men shall bolster new generations."

Antonio Ferrise suffered a severe back injury while mining in 1914, at age thirty-nine. There was no workman's compensation, disability, or welfare. While he was recovering, his son, Louis, age eleven, left school and went to work in the mines. He became the provider for his mother, father, and five siblings. His job was to guide a mule as it hauled loads of coal up and out of the mine. We don't know how much time passed until Antonio was able to go back to work. When Louis and Rose got married, some of the gifts they received were in cash. They gave the money to his parents, Antonio Ferrise and Teresa Adamo, and his twelve siblings, so they could pay some of the grocery bills at a local store. Raising a large family on a coal miner's pay was a life of poverty and debt. When Antonio died in 1940, he was still in debt to a local grocery store. A few years passed until Louis and his younger siblings, Vittoria and John, paid off the debt at the store. Four decades is a long time to be in debt.

Introduction to the letter from

Boomer, West Virginia

The writer of this letter is fifteen-year-old Louis Ferris, son of Antonio Ferrise. He is writing to his Aunt, Marianna Ferrise Loria, who is Antonio's sister. It is dated November, probably just after the war ended in 1918. Because Antonio is illiterate, he is dictating the letter to his son. Louis understands Italian but has little or no experience writing the language. Much of the text is in standard Italian, and some words are in the Calabrian dialect. He wrote what he heard, not what his father said. Consequently, the result is a heartfelt but difficult-to-read combination of misspelled words and grammatical errors. A few words are illegible, but his intent and the meaning come through.

Figure 103: Unknown child coal miner at the Turkey Knob mine Near Oak Hill West Virginia, 1908.

The subject of the letter is to inquire about his first cousins, the three Loria brothers, and to ask if they survived the war. Louis gives two cryptic hints about Fedele's brothers that deserve investigation. In the first hint, he asks if Fedele and Antonio have been liberated. In the context of war, in order to be liberated, one must first be captured. Was Antonio a POW? The second hint is when he asks if Giovanni has returned. The implication is that all three brothers were in the war. Did they serve together? These are questions without answers. Further research could result in a second edition of this book.

Figure 104: Louis Ferris

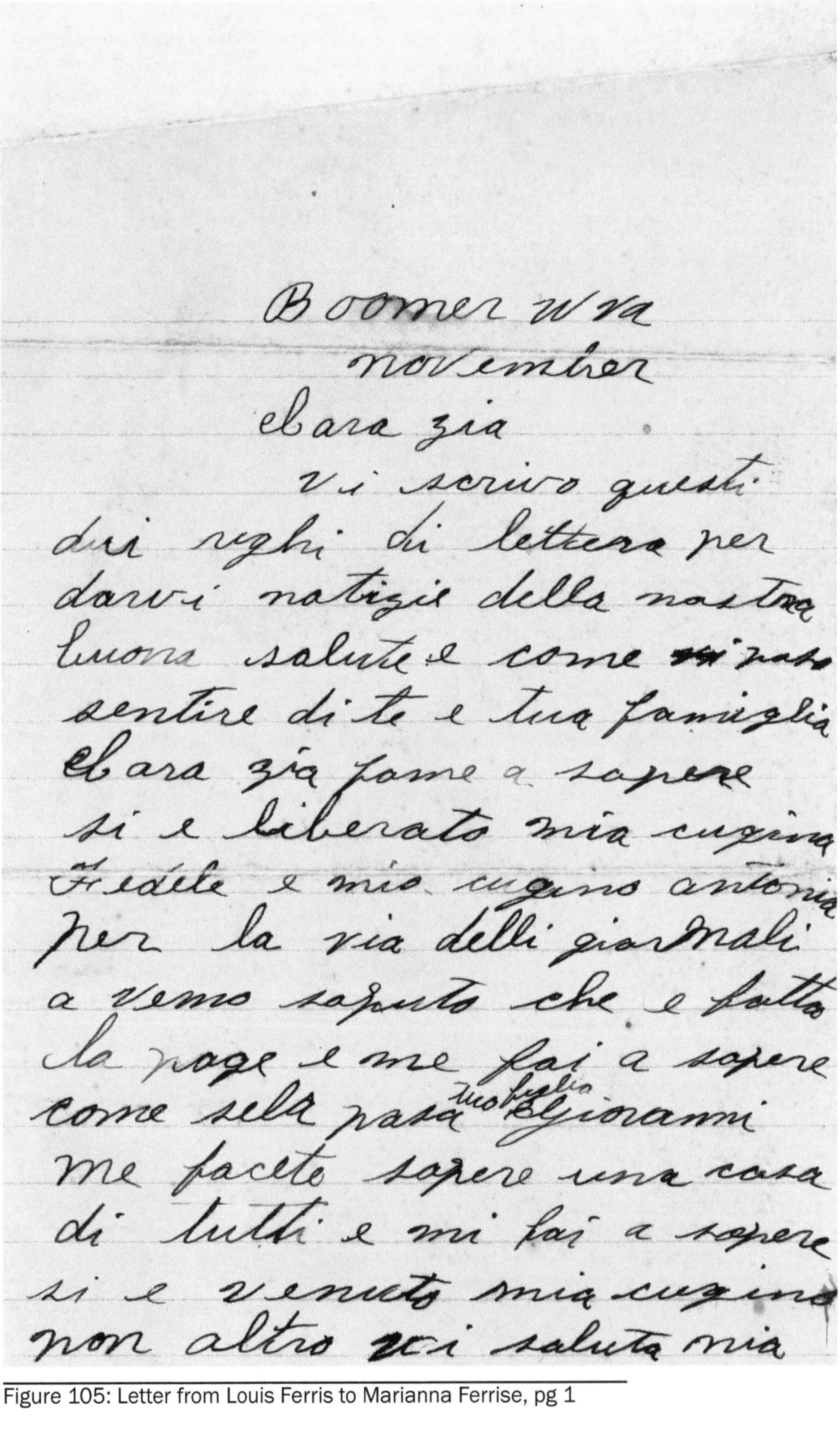

Boomer W Va

Novembre

Cara zia

vi scrivo questi

dui righi di lettera per

darvi notizie della nostra

buona salute e come pas

sentire di te e tua famiglia

Cara zia fame a sapere

si e liberato mia cugina

Fedele e mio cugino antonia

per la via delli giornali

a vemo saputo che e fatto

la pace e me fai a sapere

come sela pasa tuo figlio gioanni

me faceto sapere una cosa

di tutti e mi fai a sapere

si e venuto mia cugino

non altro vi saluta mia

Figure 105: Letter from Louis Ferris to Marianna Ferrise, pg 1

Boomer W Va

November

Dear Aunt

I am writing to you these

few lines to give you news of our

good health and ??????????[1]

to hear from you and your family

Now please let me know

If my cousin Fedele was liberated

and my cousin Antonio.

By way of the newspaper[2]

we have learned that

peace has been made. Let me

know how is you son Giovanni.

Let me know how everyone is

in your household. Let me

know if my cousin has come back.[3]

non altro ??? my mother sends greetings

to all of you

Author Commentary

1. Generally speaking, all is well with us.
2. Probably the Charleston Gazzette.
3. The cousin is probably Giovanni

nodre vi saluta mia madre
e mia zia elgiovanni vi saluta
mia sarela vataria e mia
sarela saveria e mia fratila
elgiovanni e Francesco
e vi saluto ia e saluta
al zia e vi cerco
S. B. e saluta alle mie
cugine di nuovo vi salut
e sono tua nipate
Luigi Ferrise
adio adio
buona notizie e
pronte vi risposta

Greetings to all of you from my uncle Giovanni.[1]

Greetings to all of you from my sister Vitoria

and from my sister Saveria[2]

and from my brother Giovanni

and Franceso[3]

and greetings and health to you

my aunt and I hope to see you[4]

S.B. and greetings to all of my[5]

Cousins again greeting to all of you.

I am your nephew

Luigi Ferrise[6]

Good news and

Please respond quickly

Author Commentary

1. Giovanni is to brother of Marianna and Antonio
2. Sara in English
3. Frank
4. I hope to meet you one day maybe.
5. Sua Benideta translates as: I ask for your blessing.
6. Louis Ferris

Coming and Going—A Family Affair

THE HOME OF Tomasso Loria and Marianna Ferrise was at #11 Via Vallone. Marianna's parents, Luigi Ferrise and Vittoria Olivo, lived across the street at #6 Via Vallone. Their homes were less than thirty yards from the family church of Santa Maria Della Grazie. Translated to English as Saint Mary of Grace.

During and after the war Antonio Ferrise, along with his wife, three children, and his brother Giovanni stayed in America during the war. This is likely because the brothers were too old to join the military.

Timeline

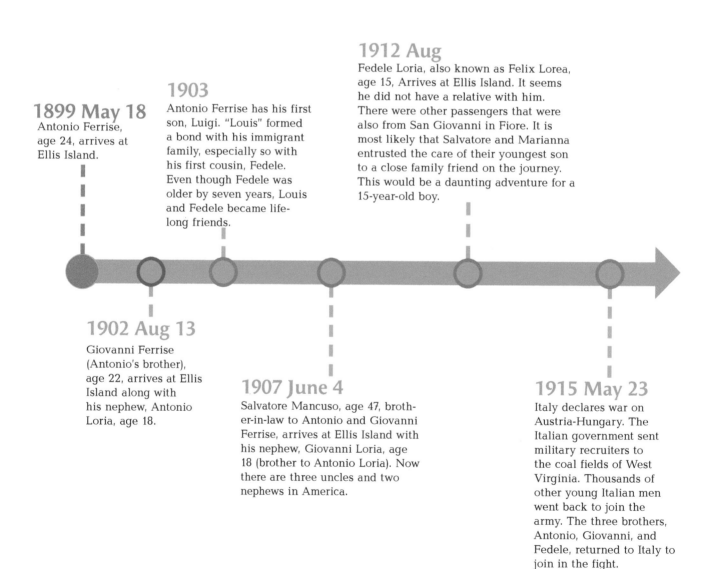

1899 May 18
Antonio Ferrise, age 24, arrives at Ellis Island.

1903
Antonio Ferrise has his first son, Luigi. "Louis" formed a bond with his immigrant family, especially so with his first cousin, Fedele. Even though Fedele was older by seven years, Louis and Fedele became life-long friends.

1912 Aug
Fedele Loria, also known as Felix Lorea, age 15, Arrives at Ellis Island. It seems he did not have a relative with him. There were other passengers that were also from San Giovanni in Fiore. It is most likely that Salvatore and Marianna entrusted the care of their youngest son to a close family friend on the journey. This would be a daunting adventure for a 15-year-old boy.

1902 Aug 13
Giovanni Ferrise (Antonio's brother), age 22, arrives at Ellis Island along with his nephew, Antonio Loria, age 18.

1907 June 4
Salvatore Mancuso, age 47, brother-in-law to Antonio and Giovanni Ferrise, arrives at Ellis Island with his nephew, Giovanni Loria, age 18 (brother to Antonio Loria). Now there are three uncles and two nephews in America.

1915 May 23
Italy declares war on Austria-Hungary. The Italian government sent military recruiters to the coal fields of West Virginia. Thousands of other young Italian men went back to join the army. The three brothers, Antonio, Giovanni, and Fedele, returned to Italy to join in the fight.

1915 Dec 12

Fedele enlists in the Italian army. It is likely that his brothers Giovanni and Antonio enlisted at about the same time.

1917 Nov 19

The battle of Caporetto, where 250,000 Italians are captured in one day.

1918 Jul 2

The last diary entry. The entries span six months and two weeks. The Lamerato sisters knew Fedele personally. Their recollection is that he was held for 5-½ months. Near the end of his diary, Fedele writes that during a period of 7 months, he received no packages.

1916 Jul 6

Fedele is wounded and captured by the Austrians. That same day he undergoes emergency surgery for abdominal wounds.

1917 Dec 12

Fedele makes the first diary entry. He was twenty-one years old.

1918 Nov 4

The war ends. If you assume he was released soon after the Austrians surrendered, he was in captivity for two years, three months, and three weeks. After the war, Fedele remained enlisted and was stationed in Milan until his discharge about 13 months later.

1919 FALL

After the war, Giovanni returned to Italy. He got married and has great-grandchildren in southern Italy. Those who returned had formed family bonds in America that were lasting and strong.

1920 May 3

Fedele (age 24) returns to America at Ellis Island along with his brother Giovanni Loria (age 29). The ship's manifest of passengers shows that Giovanni is married to Costanza, who remained in Italy. Giovanni's occupation is "reservist" in the Italian army. Sometime later, Giovanni permanently returned to his wife in Italy. Fedele never saw his family again.

1920 Jan

No doubt, all three bothers celebrated their reunion with their sisters Vittoria, Angelina, and Maria at their mother's home in San Giovanni.

1919 Dec 26

Fedele is honorably discharged with good conduct. He gave four years and two weeks of his life in service to his beloved Italy.

1924 Mar 1

Fedele gets married to Anna Marie Pedro, age 16.

Touching Tools that Touched Hearts

SOME THIRTY YEARS later, after WWII had ended, Salvatore Mancuso and the family in San Giovanni needed help because Salvatore's carpenter shop had been looted by the Germans. The family needed replacement tools to get the business going again. We believe that it was Fedele who received a letter from his uncle Salvatore asking for help. Salvatore would have to have been desperate to write such a letter. He knew the family in Boomer, West Virginia lived in poverty. He knew he was asking a lot from a coal miner with eight mouths to feed. Salvatore understood well the things family would do for family when in need. He had no doubt that his American family would come through for him. There is no living memory or record of Fedele's response to the letter, and we can only assume his role. Fedele's roots were firmly planted in his family back in San Giovanni. His love of family was strong. His response to the letter would have been a very determined will to help his uncle. Louis lived only three houses away from his cousin Fedele. Louis would have seen the letter shortly after it arrived. I am 100% sure that together, they would have made this urgent project a top priority.

What we know to be a fact is that Louis gathered up a box full of carpenter tools and had them shipped to San Giovanni. Louis had four children. In 1953, his oldest son, Anthony, was stationed in Germany. He was on leave and made a visit to San Giovanni to visit the family. Anthony could not speak Italian, and his cousins could not speak English. Salvatore's son, Francisco, and grandson, Salvatore, were very happy to take Anthony on a tour of the carpenter shop. The language barrier was overcome when they showed Anthony the well-used tools, still in the original shipping container, carefully wrapped with pages from the Charleston Gazette newspaper.

In 2019, seventy-three years later, we had a reunion with those tools. Salvatore's grandson and namesake was very happy to take us on a tour of his grandfather's old

AUTHOR'S NOTE

When Italy declared war on Austria in May of 1915, thousands of young Italian men returned to Italy to join the army. Salvatore Mancuso, Antonio, and Giovanni Loria survived the war. They went on with their lives and started families in Calabria. Salvatore started a carpentry business. Their descendants still live in San Giovanni and the surrounding areas.

shop. It had been closed and untouched in the fifty-nine years since the death of Salvatore senior in 1960. The shop is in the garage/basement of the family home at Via Fiume Lese #24. Salvatore could speak only a few words of English. We had our translator, Antonella Prosperati, but a few words of broken English and some hand gestures were all that were needed to understand one another. Present at the time were Catherine and Thresa, daughters of Louis. Also with us was Teresa Newman, granddaughter of Louis, and Patti Shears, Granddaughter of Fedele. They were able to see and touch something that usually could only be felt by the heart. As they held those tools, they were able to physically touch a memory of their loved ones. By extension of that memory, through their fingers, they touched their own roots. Words fall short of describing the depth of the feelings experienced by these women during this deeply heartfelt experience.

Figure 107: Louis Ferris, Jim Schipper, Fedele Loria. Jim Schipper was married to Vittoria Ferris, sister to Louis. Jim and Vittoria probably played a role in sending the tools to San Giovanni.

Figure 108: Salvatore Mancuso in grandfather's carpenter shop holding a photo of his grandfather, Salvatore. In the background is Antonella, Jonny Hill, Marie Hill.

Figure 109: Some of the tools on a bench

Figure 110: Salvatore senior 1872–1960. At least one of the planers in the foreground was among the tools from America. There was only one power tool in the entire shop.

Figure 111: Patti Lorea at #11 Via Vallone

Figure 112: Roger Hill with Patti Lorea Shears at the Loria home

Figure 113: Roger Hill at #6 Via Vallone, the Ferrise home.

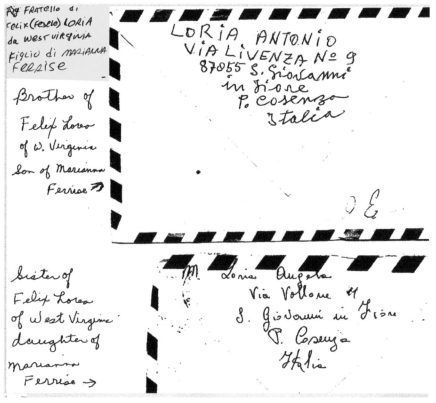

Figure 114: Return address Antonio Loria

Fedele addressed this envelope to his sister, Angela, at #11 Via Vallone. It is addressed to Signorina (unmarried) Angela Loria fu (child of) Tommaso, Town of San Giovanni in Fiore (Saint John in the Flowers), Provence of Cosenza, Via Vallone #11 (Valley Street). The envelope and letter were provided by Anna Raimondi Marazita. The Lamerato sisters provided these two envelopes that were mailed from San Giovanni to their mother.

Your Sopranome

IN SAN GIOVANNI and many other small towns in Calabria, it is customary to name the children after grandparents or their aunts and uncles. As a result, it would be common to have at least a couple of cousins with the same name. In a small town, there would not be all that many last names. Consequently, there could be confusion when talking about another person. The solution to this problem was for each family to have its own nickname. So, in effect, each person would be known by their first, last, and nickname. In Italian, this third name is called a "Sopranome." The sopranome is unofficial and usually not found on any legal documents. It is passed down in the oral tradition to the next generation. This little bit of information is practically essential when searching for family in the small towns of Calabria. The first question people will ask is, "What is your sopranome?" With time, this concept of sopranome is fading. Calabria has always been

Figure 115: Envelope addressed to Fedele's sister, Angela Loria

economically depressed. Many young people go to the industrial cities of northern Italy for employment. In the big cities, a sopranome is almost unheard of. Given a couple of more generations, this naming tradition will fade away entirely.

If you are a direct descendant of Domenico or Luigi Ferrise, then your sopranome is "Faschetta." Descendants of Salvatore/Tommaso Loria have the sopranome "Olivo." These names are hundreds of years old and are derived from the ancient Calabrian dialect. Their meanings are long lost to time. If you are a descendent of Antonio Ferrise, sopranome Faschetta, married to Thresa Adamo, then you will want to know the Adamo sopranome is "Postino," which is the Italian word for mailman. The Adamo men delivered mail for three generations that we know of, possibly more than that. Part of knowing your roots, origins, and culture is knowing your sopranome. Your ancestors were proud of the sopranome that they carried for hundreds of years. Because the use of the sopranome is fading away, you will probably never need to use it. Just by knowing your sopranome, you are preserving an ancient tradition. In this way, you give honor and respect to the name of those who came before you.

The Family Tree Abbreviated

The family tree is abbreviated because the full tree would require at least another ten pages. This book is about Fedele, his immediate family, and his descendants it is not intended to be a biography. For this reason, the tree is limited to those who are in his close family or played a significant role in his early life. Persons without a birth year were still living at the time of this book's publication. Most of the people on generation levels two through six knew him personally, or their lives were influenced by him.

With the help of our cousins in Calabria, the USA, Canada, France, and Switzerland, I have assembled a more complete family tree that contains about three hundred names. The entire tree is available for viewing at FamilySearch.org. You will need to create an account with a password. Click on-family tree, select find by ID. Enter Fedele's unique ID number, which is LTSH-3T4. Click on his name, then click on the tree symbol. For purposes of privacy, you will not be able to see the names or personal information of living persons.

Abbreviated List of Descendants of Domenico Ferrise

1 DOMENICO FERRISE ≈1813– 1861
  Spouse: Marianna Arcuri ≈ 1816–? (six children and many descendants)

    2 LUIGI FERRISE, 1824–1880
  Spouse: Vittoria Olivo 1837–1900 (six children / thirty-two grandchildren)

      3 ANTONIO FERRISE 1875–1940
  Spouse: Thresa Adamo 1882–1945 (thirteen children /Twenty grandchildren)

        4 LOUIS FERRIS 1903–1992
  Spouse: Rose Abruzzino 1909–1975 (four children / eight great grandchildren)

          5 ANTHONY FERRIS 1932–2021
  Spouse: Francis Helen French 1930–2020 (one child / three grandchildren)

          5 THRESA ANN FERRIS
  Spouse: John "Jay" William Olivero 1939–(two children / four grandchildren)

          5 KATHERINE FERRIS
  Spouse: James Kossuth 1937–2013 (two children / three grandchildren)

          5 ROSELIE FERRIS
  Spouse: Paul Price

        4 MARY ANN FERRIS 1925–2015
  Spouse: Frank B. Hill 1927–2007 (three children / four grandchildren)

          5 ROGER GEORGE HILL
  Spouse: Marie Bridges (three children)

      3 GIOVANNI FERRISE 1887–1947
  Spouse: Maria Rose Barile ?-? (four children / twenty great grandchildren)

      3 MARIA FERRISE ?–1947
  Spouse: Biagio Giramonte ?–1940 (two children / twenty-one grandchildren)

        4 Vittoria Girimonte 1903–1989
  Spouse: Salvatore "Sam" Lamerato 1899–1976 (dozens of grandchildren)

          5 ANGELINA LAMERATO
          5 VICTORIA LAMERATO
          5 ROSINA LAMERATO
          5 GINA LAMERATO

Immediate family and descendants of Fedele "Felix" Loria and Katie Pedro aka Anna Marie Patrella

3 MARIANNA FERRISE UNKNOWN DATES OF BIRTH AND DEATH

Spouse: Salvatore /Tommaso Loria 1856–?

    4 MARIA LORIA UNKNOWN DATES OF BIRTH AND DEATH

    Spouse: Salvatore Raimondi 1908–1985

        5 ANNA RAIMONDI

        Spouse: Carmine Marazita 1941–2019 (five grandchildren)

            6 CLAUDIA MARIA MARAZITA

            6 GIOVANNI MARAZITA

            Spouse: Anna Kudryashova

            6 SALVATORE MARAZITA

            Spouse: Anita Vespasiani

    4 VITTORIA LORIA

    4 ANGELINA LORIA

    4 ANTONIO LORIA ABT.1884–?

    4 GIOVANNI LORIA ABT1889–?

    Spouse: Costanza ?

    4 FEDELE "FELIX" LORIA 1896–1973

    Spouse: Anna Marie Petrella AKA Katie Pedro 1908–1997 (nine children /12 grands)

        5 SAMUEL LOREA 1928–2011

        Spouse: Olivia Geane Giannini 1933–2004

            6 PATTI LOREA

            Spouse: Dana Shears

                7 ANDREW SHEARS

            PATTI LOREA

            6 Divorced from Victor Stallard

                7 LOREA STALLARD

                Spouse: Kyle Parker

                    8 COOK LLOYDE STALLARD PARKER

            6 KATHI LOREA

            SPOUSE: MICHAEL BROWN

                7 SAMANTHA BROWN

            6 VICKY LYNN LOREA

            Spouse: Michael Bryant

                7 ALEX BRYANT

                7 EMILY BRYANT

                7 CATHERINE BRYANT

6 LISA JEAN LOREA
Spouse: James Kennedy

   7 ASHLEY KENNEDY
   7 OLIVIA KENNEDY
   7 ZACHERY KENNEDY

5 MARY LOREA LOPEZ
Spouse: Peter Lopez 1925–

5 YOLANDA LOREA 1937–1937
5 MALFALDA LOREA
5 ANGELINA LOREA 1926 –2018
5 JOHN JOSEPH LOREA 1930–2015
5 GENEVIEVE LOREA
Spouse: Harry Graves ?–2022

  6 MIKAEL GRAVES AKA BIG MIKE
  Spouse: Beth Samples

    7 MICHAEL CHRISTOPHER LEON GRAVES
  6 JOHN JOSEPH GRAVES
  Spouse: Candy Jarvis

    7 KELSEY GRAVES
    7 KALA GRAVES
    7 JOHN TAYLOR GRAVES

5 MARGUERITE LOREA
5 FRANK LOREA 1939–2018
Spouse: Nella Marie Butta

  6 STEVEN EDWARD LOREA
  Spouse: Sherry Marie Lorea

  6 ROBERT "BOBBY" PATRICK LOREA
  Spouse: Vicky Valerie Ann Webb

    7 ROBERT JORDAN LOREA
    7 JENSEN ALEXANDER LOREA
    7 JACKSON GARRETT LOREA
    7 JOSIE CLAIRE LOREA
    7 JOHN STEVEN LOREA
    7 JORGIE ISABELLA LOREA

Insights and Conclusion

I HAVE TAKEN a lot of time to think about the concept in this book and the big picture surrounding it. It seems to me that the big picture has two parts. The first and most important part is the story that Fedele told to us, his philosophy, and his legacy. The second part of that picture is my own legacy. I have never been published, nor am I rich or famous. My life has been rather unremarkable, normal by most measures. I can think of no reason to think my name or any memory of me would survive more than one or two generations after I am gone. This book is how I will be remembered long after my time on earth is completed. Eventually, this paper and ink will be dust. But in the meantime, Fedele and I will live on in this book.

I am not writing this book for money. I can safely say that this will be a money-losing venture. I simply do not care about the money. There are a few endeavors in life where the analysis of cost and benefit simply do not apply, and this book is one of them. The effort and time to write this book is a reward in itself. I have invested hundreds and hundreds of hours in researching Fedele, his life, and the places and events he mentions in his diary. The reward far exceeds the cost of time, effort, and expense to write this book. In this journey, I have learned so much about our far-flung family.

The priority in my life is the health and welfare of my wife, Marie, and our children, Joe and Jonny. Everything that I do revolves around or relates to their well-being. This is what a good husband and father does. I do these things not from obligation but from love. They own my unending loyalty. My love of family extends far beyond them. This love of family, near and far, is my life's passion. If you are lucky enough to have found your passion, then you will not need an explanation as to why I have dedicated thousands of hours of my time to establishing and cultivating relationships with our far-flung family of immigrants. My outreach to our cousins has been universally well-received. Some were hesitant at first. They probably wondered who is this person, Roger Hill? "He says we are cousins, I never heard of him." Eventually, they would come around to accept me. To many, it was a complete surprise to realize that they do, in fact, have second and third cousins on different continents. You could say that on a few occasions, I created a stir in some of these distant family groups. These efforts to reach out to distant family and to cultivate relationships have been a journey of discoveries, too many to mention here. In brief, I can say that the love we felt from our long-lost and new-found family in Italy can be summed up like this.

They received us with open arms as if we were long lost and returning royalty.

I have reestablished connections with our family on five continents, in nine countries. In our family, we speak at least six different languages. My address book lists 130 households representing about 500 of our living blood relatives. For me, Christmas cards are not a chore, they are a pleasure. I send them out in late October, and by Christmas, I will receive replies from all over the world.

Along the way, in cultivating and developing these relationships, I have learned a great deal about myself. I found my passion, and I love it. I am a kind of ambassador. To many, I represent the American branch of the family. I receive a great deal of satisfaction when I can do something like helping our family in Argentina to reconnect with their long-lost relatives in Calabria. Over a period of years, I have become the unofficial, self-appointed ambassador for the family. It gives me great pleasure, and it is something that I am honored to do. One day, someone will pick up this torch and carry it on for the next generation. But for now, I intend to carry that torch high and pursue this passion for as long as I live.

I remember the day that I learned of Fedele's diary. At that moment, I knew I wanted to translate it into English. Fedele has several grandchildren here in America. They were so surprised to learn about this chapter of his life. Most of them did not know that he was a prisoner, and none of them knew about the diary or his combat wounds. Each of them told me this book would be a treasured heirloom to be passed on to the next generations. It was becoming apparent to me just how important a translation would be to them and their descendants. I had no idea what a great adventure this project would become. My initial intention to do a simple translation has evolved into an endeavor that has, in part, become my legacy. Fedele's story is the focus, of course, but my name will be on the cover of the book about his book.

The time and effort I have put into this book have brought some rewards to me. But my ultimate reward lies not between the covers of this book or in the journey I have experienced. The ultimate reward will take about 100 years to realize. I hope the day will come when my great-grandchild believes that his son or daughter is old enough to understand the value of his or her culture, history, and origins. On the day that my great-grandchild passes this book to the next generation, I will have my ultimate reward. Then I will know that my efforts to write this book, and my life, had meaning to the generations beyond me.

Now that we have read his story, we have an insight into this period of Fedele's life. He told us about the things that were important to him. We can see the sacrifices he made for God, country, and family. His words have given us some perspective on the sequence of events that shaped the philosophy of life.

Consider taking some time to reflect on your own life. What shapes you and your philosophy? Here is something to consider. Know your roots. Know yourself. Find your passion. Then you can leave a legacy.

More than thirteen million Italians came to America. They made an uncountable number of sacrifices to seek a better life. Each generation should be given the opportunity to understand and appreciate the sacrifices made by their immigrant ancestors. Fedele came to America so that he and his descendants would have a chance at the American Dream.

We owe it to him to remember his name, his life, and his story.

Acknowledgments

FEDELE'S GREAT NEPHEW, **Salvatore Marazita**, provided the translation of Canzonetta Funebre, which is literally translated as *Little funeral song*. Salvatore speaks three languages: standard Italian, English, and Calabrian dialect. Writing poetry with rhythm and meter requires shortening or adapting words, sometimes combining words in an unusual sequence. Being trilingual allowed him to understand Fedele's unique combination of adjectives and verbs. He was able to understand and explain nuances in detail that others did not observe.

Figure 116: The Marazita Family in Rende, Italy. The 50th wedding anniversary of Anna and Carmine 2016. Back row left: Gabriele, Salvatore, Anna, Carmine, Marazita, Anna Kudryashova, Maria Claudia Marazita, Anita Vespasiani, Giovanni Marazita. Front row left: Matteo Marazita, Carlotta Apicella, Livia Marazita, Valeria Marazita.

Figure 117: Roger Hill and Anna Marazita at La Duchessa Della Sila Hotel. San Giovanni in Fiore, 2017. The diary, photos, and postcards are on her lap.

Figure 118: The Hill family 2016: Roger, Joe, Marie, Jonny

Figure 119: Family reunion at Casa Lopez, San Giovanni in Fiore 2019. Left: Anna Raimondi Marazita, Patti Lorea and Dana Shears, Maria Claudia Marazita.

Figure 120: From top: Paul Price, Roselie Ferris,
Francis French, Anthony Ferris, Kathryn Ferris, Jim
Kossuth, Thresa Ferris, and John "Jay" Oliverio.

Figure 121: The Lorea Family 2022. Back row left: Jack, Valerie, Bob, Jordan, Aeris. Front row left: Jensen, Jorgie, Josie, John.

Fedele's grandson, **Bobby Lorea**, was key to understanding a phrase that simply has no translation. In the chapter "My Vacation in the Trenches," Fedele uses the words "dum dum . . . ". At least a dozen people were puzzled by these words. Bobby solved the mystery in just a few minutes. Thank you, Bobby, for your insight into the world of munitions. To see the meaning of those words, you will need to read that chapter. Bobby came through again with the research he did on mustard gas. He deeply loved his grandfather. By doing this research on munitions and mustard gas, Bobby honors Fedele's name, memory, and legacy his grandfather left us. One day, in conversation with Bobby, he summed up this book in just a few sentences. He said, "And think how powerful this knowledge is. From here forward, we must stop and think. Fedele didn't dig turnips out of trash cans, climb the alps taking enemy fire, lay fallen and bloodied, and then survive a German concentration camp just so I could complain about slow internet, or traffic, or any one of a million petty things that cause people to throw up their hands and quit today. He took us places from humble beginnings in San Giovanni, didn't he?"

Figure 122: Vittoria Lamerato

The Lamerato sisters—Gina, Angelina, Vicky, and Rose—are the daughters of Salvatore "Sam" Lamerato of San Giovanni in Fiore and Hamtramck, Michigan. Sam was married to Fedele's first cousin, Vittoria Giramonte. Sam and Fedele were lifelong friends and confidants. The sisters were able to relate to me their memories of Fedele. With the oral history they passed on to me, we were able to preserve some of the history of Fedele's time in captivity. Their recollection is that he was held for 5-½ months. According to the 1920 census and the sisters' recollection, Fedele and Sam worked as miners and lived in Logan, WV.

Sam assisted Fedele in obtaining his military service awards and military pension. When Sam and Vittoria celebrated their 50th wedding anniversary, Fedele was the best man at the renewal of their wedding vows. Fedele was godfather to their daughter Mary. Many times, the families traveled between Boomer, West Virginia and

Hamtramck, MI, for vacation visits. Early in 1973, Fedele received his cancer diagnosis. During Fedele's last months, Gina drove her father, Sam, from Michigan to West Virginia to visit his old friend. She recalls them sitting on the porch swing, "Just talking while holding hands." He stayed with Fedele for a couple of months before their final goodbye.

Figure 123: Gina Lamerato

Figure 124: FatherAnthonyFortunato

A Catholic priest in the Order of the Blessed Virgin Mary of Mercy, **Father Anthony Fortunato**, known to his friends as 'Father Tony,' is a native of Calabria. He used his eighty-plus years of experience and his knowledge of the Calabrian dialect to decipher the poem *Spinci Spinci ame*.

Father Tony gave me valuable insight as to what Fedele was really trying to say. With Father's help, the chapter "Canzonetta delle Donne" *Little Song of the Women* is more clearly understood, because it contains a few nuances and subtleties that are not obvious to a casual reader.

The poem *Orfanella Senza Tennto*, translated as *Homeless Orphan*, is, in part, a fervent and humble prayer. Father Tony was the perfect person to interpret Fedele's thoughts and intentions in this prayer. My thanks go out to you, Father Tony, for all your help.

Figure 125: Lorea Stallard, legislative assistant to Vice President Air Force 2

Lorea Stallard received her bachelor's degree in history from Appalachian State and her Juris Doctor degree from the University of North Carolina at Chapel Hill. She became a Special Assistant for Legislative Affairs in the office of Vice President Joe Biden. Her duties involved meetings with V.P. Biden and staffing him when he met with senators and members of congress. On several occasions, she accompanied him on Air Force 2.

Figure 127: Beverly Ferris Davison with Jonny Hill during the family reunion at Casa Lopez, 2017.

Figure 126: Antonella Prosperati

Antonella Prosperati said to me, "The real gold in Calabria lies in the heart of its people." The golden heart of Calabria beats strong in her. She is *Calabrese vero (real Calabrian).* Few love our common heritage more than she does. Antonella is a freelance author /tour guide/English teacher /translator/and more. Her specialty is in helping Americans of Italian heritage to find their roots. She is the reason we were able to find our living relatives in Calabria. Finding our relatives eventually led to bringing Fedele's diary out of a closet and into your hands. If you would like to contact her, she can be found on Facebook. I cannot thank her enough for the difference she has made in the lives of myself and our family.

Figure 128: Jesse Davison

Figure 129: Anna Silvestri and her sister, Maddelena Clemente, at Casa del Pane.

My friends at La Casa Del Pane, *House of Bread*, have an authentic Italian deli /espresso bar. **Anna Silvestri** and her sister **Maddalena Clemente** are such gracious hostesses. They have created a warm and inviting atmosphere that is a favorite among the local Italians. The "big table" is a communal gathering place to break bread and taste a bit of "The Old Country." This is where my Italian friends and I had espresso and cannoli while deciphering Fedele's style of old-world handwriting. Anna's husband, **Gianni**, is the baker. You can get good bread in Italy, or you can come to "Casa" to get great bread! La Casa Del Pane is on St. Pete Beach in Florida.

Figure 130: Marco Tavola doing some translation of the diary at the big table in Casa del Pane.

Marco Tavola is a long-time friend of the Silvestri family at Casa Del Pane. He was able to assist in the translation of some difficult-to-understand passages. Marco is a free-lance tour guide in Rome and much of Italy.

You can contact Marco by e-mail at: Marcoprivatetours@gmail.com.

Figure 131: Aldo Feretti

As native Italian speakers, **Aldo Ferretti, Dominico Staganelli, Daniela Frugis, Rita Gallace Congiu, and Mario Congiu** were essential for the translation to English. These friends were able to read and understand those idiomatic expressions, misspelled words, and phrases in a Calabrian dialect that otherwise was impossible for me to understand. They share a background in Catholicism with Fedele, which allowed them to shed light on some traditions and customs that are not well-known

here in America. However, even these Italian friends found Fedele's writing difficult to read and even more difficult to understand. Aldo served in the Italian army. That experience gave him valuable insight into the references to military life and weapons mentioned in the diary. Fedele wrote in long hand script with a quill pen on paper that has been fading for one hundred and five years. Dominico is the host of an Italian radio talk show. He has a broad knowledge of Italian culture and a command

Figure 132: Daniella Frugis

Figure 133: Rita Gallace Congiu

of the language. This expertise allowed him to interpret and explain the nuances of Fedele's writing. Daniela was up to the challenge of translating his handwriting. She gave at least ninety hours of determined effort at my side as we struggled to decipher his cryptic style of writing, sometimes one letter at a time. Rita and her husband Mario are from Calabria. When Rita read the poem Spinci Spinci ami, long-forgotten memories came to her. The poem reminded her of songs her grandmother sang to her when she was a child. Her childhood memories gave her insight into the childlike and playful nature of the poem. When interpreted literally, it is very difficult to understand. Her childhood memories were essential because Spinci Spinci ami is a metaphorical depiction of his life to this point. Without all of my Italian friends, this book would never have been written.

Figure 134: Mario Congiu

Anna P. Zurzolo is an accomplished author who was kind enough to share a few pearls of wisdom about how to publish a successful first book. In addition to being a kind person, she is a mother of two, an accomplished businesswoman, and the author of the very popular book *Bread Wine and Angels*. Anna was raised in San Giovanni in Fiore. Her book about life and lessons learned in Calabria is timeless. For those of us who have origins in San Giovanni, this book is essential reading. It can be found on Amazon, ISBN 0−88801-213−6. Because she is a native speaker, Anna was able to assist in translating Fedele's letter, "Coming Home Soon." Thank you, Anna.

Figure 135: Anna Zurzolo

Sandra Brodney, Ph.D. has been a national board-certified teacher since 2001. She has authored numerous papers on subjects of science and math, at the state and national level. Dr. Brodney has thirty-nine years of teaching experience ranging from elementary to graduate level instruction. Sandra's background perfectly qualifies her to advise this novice writer on how to craft a coherent and engaging story. I am fortunate to have her as a friend and advisor. Thank you, Sandi

Steve Michael Graves, Fedele's grandson, played a key role in gathering Fedele's documents, such as his passport, military records, and other helpful information.

Figure 136: Robert Jacob

Robert and Anne Jacob have guided this novice writer through the confusing number of ways to write and publish a book. Rob is an award-winning author and president of the Florida Authors and Publishers Association (FAPA). Rob retired as a Chief Warrant Officer 5 from the United States Marine Corps. His military background perfectly qualified him to write part of the chapter, 12 Battles of the Isonzo River. Additionally, he scanned and formatted the digital images of the historical documents, including the diary pages. His wife, Anne, is the editor of this book and serves on the FAPA board of directors. They were willing to share their expertise to help me climb the learning curve of how to publish my first book. I am sure this book would have been amateurish at best without their help.

Figure 137: Anne Jacob

Figure 138: Dawn Sheddon

Professor Dawn Shedden, PhD, made valuable contributions by drawing on her extensive knowledge of nineteenth and twentieth-century European history. She added insight into the background of political and social events that shaped Europe prior to and during the Great War. Dawn has a broad knowledge of German, Spanish, French, and Italian languages. Her background in German studies was especially helpful in translating Fedele's medical records that were written in German.

My friend, **Martin Flügel**, made valuable contributions while interpreting Fedele's medical chart, which was written in German. Martin is from a small town near Frankfurt. He became fluent in English because it was one of his favorite subjects in high school. With his bilingual skills, he was able to fine-tune our interpretation of Fedele's medical records. Martin is a mechanical engineer in Frankfurt, Germany. Thank you, Martin

Figure 139: Roger Hill and Martin Flügel

Writing this book has been a collaborative effort. How could I ever thank all those who helped? I could never have done it all by myself.

Index

D

E

F

G

H

I

L

M

machine guns 50, 135

Map. *See*
  Italy 196
  Italy, Austria, and Solvenia 162
  Boomer and surrounding towns 204
  West Virginia 203

Mauthausen Concentration Camp 11, 14–15, 136, 153. *See also* concentration camp

model 1891 55

Monfalcone 63, 71

Monongah 206–8

Mt. Saint Busi 51

Mustard gas 66

O

Olivo 214, 223–4

P

Postino 223

S

Saint Lucia 71

Saint Mary 71, 194, 214

San Giovanni in Fiore 1, 64, 176, 192–3, 196–8, 205, 207–8, 214, 222, 230–1, 234, 241

San Martino 71

San Michael 71

Santa Maria 51, 59, 132, 194, 214

Sigmundscherberg 9

Printed in the USA
CPSIA information can be obtained
at www.ICGtesting.com
LVHW071513091023
760506LV00059B/212